Axis Stone Mysteries

SMUGGLER'S HOLE

G. L. Keady

Big Island Productions
PO Box 3027, Tuross Head, 2537, NSW, Australia.
www.bigislandprod.net

ISBN:
E-book: 978-1-923038-05-9
Print: 978-1-923038-04-2

Edited by: Canon Doyle
Cover design and art: Brandon Evans-Keady

TABLE OF CONTENTS

CHAPTER ONE

I **WOKE UP** in a deathly dark space and groaned through parched and swollen lips, "Am I dead?" I tried my best, hog-tied in a foetal position, to roll over. To my relief, a couple of tiny dust-filled ribbons of light coursing through pinholes in the ceiling eased my claustrophobia. The cramped space told me I was locked in the trunk of a car. My head was throbbing, not from booze or drugs but from having been belted. My mouth tasted like the floor of a cocky's cage, and then there was the scorching heat... it was like an oven. I needed to get untied and out before I ended up like a Sunday roast. A thought flashed in my mind — I remembered a brunette and being on the floor of her pad. My survival instincts kicked in, and I flicked the thought. Figuring if I concertina my legs, I might be able to kick the lid open. Sweating like a pig, after a struggle, I manoeuvred into position to give it my best mule kick, but before I let it go, the trunk flew open of its own accord, sending blinding light flooding in. With my wrists bound together held up in front of my face to shield my eyes, through the glare, I watched a distorted black, withered arm reach in and like the proverbial hand of God, offer me the way out.

As my saviour untied me, wavering groggily with blurred vision, all became clear. I was surrounded by a vista of red desert and a rich blue sky that met it on a lateral horizon. Standing amidst the vision like a craggy old leafless tree was an Aboriginal. A bearded jaw with the rest of the face painted with white dots and dashes, long white hair, skinny legs, and bare feet, his wise old tell-tale eyes glared at me like I'd just teleported from an alternative metaverse. I opened my mouth to speak, but all that came out was a cough and a croak, and then, "Ahem, thanks man, I owe you big time. How the hell did you know I was in there?"

A stave in one hand, garbed in a dark red wrap with a colourful fabric bag strung over one bare bony shoulder, he fired me a big partially toothless grin and then admitted, "Could smell ya."

"Hmm, must've been the aftershave," I returned in defence of my dignity.

He cracked a smile. "Plenty of trouble for you, white fella... if you stay here, you'll croak... blow-up full of bloody maggots."

"Yeah, well, I'm sure you're right about that, mate. Anyhow, I'm Axis Stone, and you are?"

"Kokatha mob."

"So, where's the rest of the Kokatha mob?" I said, glancing at the rusted-out old derelict shell of a car riddled with bullet holes I'd been holed up in.

"Over there, Konening Lake, you white fellas call Lake Torrens. That-a-way," he said, pointing at a different spot on the horizon only visible to him. "Andamooka."

It all looked like desert to me.

"You Yankee. What are you doing here?"

"Took the wrong turn at the New Jersey Turnpike, I guess," I joked, mostly to myself, not expecting him to get the gag.

"That some kinda Yankee talk?"

I chuckled. "Yeah, not my best gag. No, I'm from Sydney but maybe spent a bit of time over there."

I got an idea and pulled my cellphone from my back pocket.

The old man pointed at it and cackled, "No bloody signal out here, fella."

I hadn't expected him to be hip to technology. "Naturally," I agreed, then snapped a shot of the derelict car. "How far is

Andamooka? I'm staying at the hotel." I aimed my phone at him to get a photo, but when he held up a hand, I declined.

He threw out a long scrawny arm with a pointed finger and growled, "Andamooka, ten miles as the crow flies that-a-way." Then he looked down at the ground. "You follow them tyre tracks, see?"

"Last time I looked, I wasn't a crow. Mate, I'll die walking for ten miles in this heat without water."

"Plenty of water round here, mate, no worries," he said matter-of-factly. "Anyhow, that's about all the free advice."

That threw me. "Free?" I squawked. "But I need help."

He showed me the palm of his hand. "Everyone needs help, brother."

I thought to myself, just my luck, an entrepreneurial saviour with a sense of humour. "Don't suppose you take Amex?" I asked cynically.

Shaking his head, he grumbled, "Nar, don't be ridiculous... merchant fee too high."

I tried to barter, "How about my watch, then?"

"Don't have time for one. Tell you what, I'll give you a freebie. See that plant over there, the one with little white flowers?" He pointed at it.

My mind flashed on the healing properties of Chinese White Flower oil. "Yes?"

"Well, don't eat that shit, it'll kill ya."

"Oh, thanks," I said with a gulp, then with sarcasm added, "You do stand-up comedy as well, do you?"

"See the other one, yellow flower?"

It was a small flat weed. Expecting another gag, I muttered pensively, "Yeah?"

"You pull it out, chew the root, makes you pee. When thirsty, rip off some shirt, pee on it, then suck it. Tastes crook but saves you. You better rip some shirt off to cover your white scalp anyhow, or it'll cook. Get grease from axle under the car, or your silly white face will blister like a barbecued pig," he chuckled.

I motioned at the old wreck, "Ah, come on, man, there wouldn't be any grease left on that burnt-out old thing." He gave me a glum look, so I dropped to my knee and peered underneath. "Well, I'll be! Goddamn, you're right... there's grease near the sump." There was just enough space to crawl underneath. I smeared the smelly black grease on my face and then slid back out. "How's that?" I said, glancing up at the old man. "Uh?" I grunted, he'd vanished. Back on my feet, I scanned the topography for him. Way in the distance shimmered a black speck; it had to be him, but how? Bizarre, I thought, then started to walk. As instructed, I ripped the tail off my favourite Pink Floyd T-shirt, draped it over my head, and then followed the barely visible tyre tracks. By my calculation, it would take three hours to get to town if the trek didn't kill me first.

While trudging along, I recalled how I got into this mess in the first place.

It all began with sexy Sherri Sun, the miraculous masseuse who had been staying with me since the end of the last case. The recollection flooded back with distasteful alarming clarity. Funny how the mind works; the first thing was the song "Foul Play" blasting from my sound system, a song that will now forever be linked to Sherri Sun and that particular unsavory episode in my Sydney apartment.

We were having an argument. Well, to be precise, Sherri was having an argument, and I was silently bearing the brunt. I had learned pretty quickly that Sherri was equipped with a serious temper, a stinger in her tail, and a penchant for throwing stuff to emphasize a point. She needed to scream to compete with the volume of the music, and that made her even more animated. I can't remember what had ticked her off, but she was probably accusing me of being a narcissist. Such was the general theme of contention from women I had tried to cohabit with. Ultimately, they would become confused between my overt self-confidence and egotism, which over time, say a couple of weeks, would begin to irk them... in the same way an unpalatable habit such as leaving the toilet seat up can. There was a litany of absurdities about the horribly one-sided argument.

As she was screaming and carrying on in a furore, I was beginning to look at her through a different lens, thinking perhaps this was the real Sherri. Then I noticed her lips were moving, mouthing superlatives to the max that I wasn't hearing. I reclined in my armchair and watched her freak out like it was a scene in some sicko TV soap opera, thinking, 'How can a woman love you one minute then hate you the next?'

Her eyes suddenly flashed on me as though she was reading my mind, and then sharply focused on the coffee table upon which sat an empty bottle of JD from the night before. I quickly snatched it before she could use it as a weapon... then she turned her attention to my 1966 Fender Stratocaster in its stand, an innocent bystander to the altercation. Absolute dread consumed me. Her eyes narrowed fierce and feral, and she went for it. I bounced out of the chair like my life depended on it and took up a position like a colossus in front of my most treasured possession.

Desperate to destroy something precious to me, she changed tack, targeted the bookcase, and fastened her claws around the spine of "Hades' Daughter" by Sara Douglass. How fitting, I thought. Sara came flying at me. I ducked, and it crashed into the rack-mounted stereo system. "Foul Play" stopped abruptly as though its throat had been cut.

Sherri froze, thinking she'd busted the stereo, and burst into tears. However, what I'd perceived as regret was short-lived. She promptly transformed into a screaming skull with, "Go to hell, Axis Stone!"

And with that, Sherri Sun, my lovely Tantric masseuse who had convinced me she had no inner demons, stormed out, slamming her chapter in my biography shut behind her. Somehow, I'd survived her tirade and thought, I can't blame her, I guess — I'm a total cow to live with and maybe just a smidgen narcissistic — guilty as accused — however, I reckon that comes with the good looks.

After a week, I started missing Sherri, so to avoid groveling, I decided to distract myself and headed to the office for the first time in ages. I was pretty cashed up after the shark-leg case, so there was no motivation to rush into the next gig. I found a message from my mate Nick on my vintage '70s answering machine, reminding me about the bloke he'd recommended who needed some help, and I thought I may as well give him a courtesy call on the number provided.

After a short chat, he seemed like a nice enough bloke, and it just so happened he was in town, so we agreed to catch up for a coffee at my favorite breakfast haunt, The Grind Café, conveniently located next door to Regal Apartments in Sussex Street, where I lived.

I was sipping on a double-shot espresso when two guys walked into the café and asked if I was Axis Stone. Turns out, they were brothers, Rod and Gary. It was Rod that Nick had originally met in a pub in Winton, western Queensland, where he was looking to buy an opal for his girl, Kitty Lovejoy. Rod is a Sydney-based opal dealer, while Gary, the elder of the two, is an author who lives down the South Coast of New South Wales.

After the obligatory preamble, I asked, "So, Rod, did Nick end up buying an opal for Kitty?"

"No, it's not that easy to find a good stone in the bush these days, but I've got a stock of them. I'll give him a look next time he comes to town. He'll be able to pick one up from me much cheaper than he could buy from retail," Rod said blithely.

"Good-o," I said, turning my gaze to his brother. "Nick mentioned you might need some help, Gary?"

The guy looked worried. It was a look I've seen plenty of times before on people in trouble. Rod gave him a comforting nod, and he spoke up, somewhat timidly.

"I... I've had an heirloom for the best part of fifty years that I decided recently to liquidate, to buy a new house. You know how it is; I'd turned seventy and felt it was time for a sea-change. But first, I needed someone to sell the stone for me overseas. Rod suggested a bloke from Andamooka—"

Rod recognised the mystified expression on my face and explained, "Andamooka is an opal-mining town in South Australia... the guy had sold stones for me before, a sales agent per se."

"He was coming through Sydney on his way to the States on a selling trip, so we hooked up."

I butted in. "What was the item?"

"Sorry, we should've said, it's a twenty-five-carat Queensland boulder opal, named The Pride of Queensland," Rod answered for his brother.

I knew nothing about opals, so I asked, "Pardon my ignorance, but what's a stone like that worth?"

"At least a quarter of a million US," Rod said.

"Well, that's how much it should've been insured for," Gary glumly admitted.

I cleared my throat... it was a lot of money. "Go on," I said easily.

I could tell Gary was doing it tough; he sighed heavily and then continued. "This bloke said he might have a customer for it in the States, so I agreed to give it to him on consignment."

"Consignment means...?" I queried.

"Oh, a written guarantee or a contract if you like, stating he'd return the stone within thirty days if he doesn't sell it. It also contains the terms of sale," Rod explained.

"A commission?" I queried.

"Yes, we haggled over that, but we finally agreed on fifteen percent of the sale price," Gary muttered remorsefully.

"Whoa, a cool thirty-seven thousand bucks, not too shabby for one quick deal," I cracked, wishing something like that would drop into my lap once in a while. "So, cut to the chase."

Gary looked too uncomfortable to continue, so Rod took over. "He sold it to a film producer."

"Good-o, then what?" I quizzed, buying into the yarn. "Don't tell me he ran off with the bread?"

"No, he delivered the stone, took a ten percent cash deposit, and a promissory note for the remainder," Gary said dourly. "Which subsequently bounced like a bloody basketball after I deposited it in the bank here."

"Nothing worse," I grumbled, reclining in my chair and eyeballing Gary. "Did you call the Feds?"

"No," he answered sharply.

"Why the hell not?" I snarled.

"Look, when we pushed Kovacs..." Gary started.

Rod cut in to clarify, "That's the name of the guy from Andamooka... Josh Kovacs. You've got to understand, selling an opal that size is a difficult proposition—"

Gary cut him off irritably, "Kovacs went to ground, won't even take our calls."

"Did you get your claws on the deposit?" I asked.

"No, he kept it, claiming it barely covered his expenses," Gary complained.

"Sounds like a scammer," I hissed. "So, what do you think I can do?"

They exchanged a look of desperation; it seemed they were at their wits' end with Kovacs.

"Wait," I said. "You mentioned insurance... was it covered?"

"No, it would have cost too much to insure. As well as that, we think Kovacs would've smuggled the stone into the States to avoid paying import duty," Rod admitted.

It was getting more and more complicated.

"Well, that's a bloody good reason for not calling in the Feds," I pressed.

"This bastard Kovacs has totally clammed up on us... won't tell us anything," Gary growled, while nervously wringing his hands.

"That's only because he's trying to hang onto the deposit," Rod countered angrily. "I feel guilty because I recommended the guy."

"Argh, don't say that, bro. You weren't to know," Gary corrected him.

It was easy to see by their exchange how much the brothers cared for each other. I reclined in my chair, drained my coffee, and then said pessimistically, "Look, I don't know, fellas, this really isn't my cup of tea." I was telling the truth. It was a case for an ex-cop—a PI with more experience in fraud than me. I'm a bloke better skilled at catching adulterous husbands and wives.

"Why is that? Nick told me you were the best in the game," Rod said, a little surprised.

I figured their backs were against the wall... I was probably their last hope. "Look," I started plaintively, "two things bother me: one, the costs—by the sound of it, I'd need to go to Andamooka to question Kovacs, and then to the States to talk to the customer—and two, I don't have any connections in the States. Do you know where this producer is located?"

"Yes, Hollywood," Gary confirmed.

Well, that stood to reason, and didn't that word just resonate with adventure—I thought to myself, don't talk yourself out of this one, buddy, you could do with some fun.

"We'll pay your way to Andamooka. If you get what's left of the deposit from Kovacs, it'll cover a trip to the States. If you get the money for the stone, I'll give you the commission we offered Kovacs, less the deposit, of course," Gary rattled off the deal like it was premeditated.

I studied their faces, wondering if I trusted them. "Tell you what," I concluded, "let me sleep on it. I'll let you know one way or the other in the morning. Fair enough?"

They both nodded reservedly.

CHAPTER TWO

DON'T ASK ME why, but something about this case tickled my fancy. Maybe the thought of going to Sin City: Hollywood. I rang the guys in the morning and agreed to the deal. I got what I needed from them over the phone, and by noon, I was on a flight to Adelaide, the capital of South Australia.

Standing at the Adelaide Airport cab rank, my ringtone, 'The Terrible Tango,' broke the silence. At the other end was the voice of my buddy Nick Vargas, who had originally recommended me for the case. "Hey Nick, how goes it, mate? Where are you?"

"Brisbane," his Filipino-accented voice answered. "You?"

"Just landed in Adelaide, about to hop in a taxi to Parafield Airport for a charter flight to Andamooka."

"Anda-whatta?"

"Andamooka. It's an old opal mining town six hundred clicks north of here...in the desert."

"I confess, Axis, I know what you're up to, buddy. I just got off the phone with Rod, he filled me in."

"Yeah, well, as you should know, it's not the sort of case I generally take, but..."

"Ah, crap man," he jumped in. "It's right up your alley...weird, and in Hollywood, Sin City!...Ha! Pull the other one. Look, I haven't met his brother Gary, but if Rod's an indicator, I'm sure you can trust them, as honest as the day is long, so they say up here in Queensland."

"Mate, you've only been in Brisbane a month or two, and you're already sounding like a banana bender! Next, you'll be swearing like a trooper and drinking four X beer."

"Is that what they call Queenslanders? Banana benders?" he chuckled. "No, I'm still a Pinoy to the core."

"Good-o, I'll give you a call from Andamooka if there's a signal that side of the black stump."

"The black stump?" he queried. "Is that nearby?"

"Sorry, mate, it's Aussie slang. It means a bloody long way from anywhere or anything."

"I'll remember that. Sounds like this guy you're going to meet is a loose cannon. Be careful, my friend."

"Not likely to get into any trouble out there, mate. The population will tick over to four hundred and one when I arrive," I joked.

"While one of the four hundred wears a skirt and is under thirty-five with a halfway decent body, there's trouble waiting for you to happen, my friend," he chuckled knowingly.

"Mate, since Rosy, Jazz, Suzie, and then Sherri, with emphasis on the last one, I'm over females for a while."

"What happened with Sherri? Isn't she a Tantric Buddhist, you know, peace-loving...?"

"She turned on me...they all do eventually," I said forlornly. "So, an overnight stay, and I'm out of Andamooka."

"We'll see about that. I know you, Axis. Anyhow, as always, yell out if you need me. Take care, Kemosabe."

I took a cab for the forty-minute drive to the light aircraft facility at Parafield. I had timed it perfectly: the plane I had chartered was fuelled up and ready to fly. It was my first time sitting up front next to the pilot in a light aircraft. The Beechcraft Baron would get us to Andamooka in a couple of hours. Floyd Truffle, the pilot, assured me of a relatively smooth flight, as he forecasted clear skies.

Flying at ten thousand feet in clear air gave us a bird's-eye view of the country, and Floyd didn't miss an opportunity to point out features along the way. He was a bit of a topography nerd. I absorbed geographical trivia that I would probably never have any use for.

After a couple of hours of intelligent conversation with Floyd on subjects ranging from politics to aliens, airplanes, and COVID conspiracies, I became a bit nervous when he suddenly pushed the stick forward to perform aerial acrobatics, buzzing the tiny town of Andamooka to signal our impending landing. It was a display of true bush pilot skills.

Flying at about three hundred feet, Floyd grinned and said, "This'll scare 'em off." I craned my neck to look wide-eyed out of the window and saw a mob of emus on the dirt runway below. We swooped hair-raisingly low to scare them off. I almost threw up my breakfast, and Floyd noticed the colour drain from my face. He immediately ended the joy ride, circled around, and prepared for landing. Though it wasn't my cup of tea, I must admit his precision flying was impressive. He landed the plane smoothly, without so much as a bump, and taxied up to the terminal.

We climbed out into the scorching atmosphere, which seemed to instantly drain every ounce of water from our bodies through our armpits, leaving us feeling dehydrated within minutes. Floyd locked up the plane, and we walked to the terminal, each with our ports in hand. The terminal was a tin shed. It was then that I realised, as far as the eye could see, the land was as flat as a pancake, with us likely being the only human inhabitants for miles.

Floyd announced, "Reckon that dust-devil over there is our ride to town."

I scanned the horizon through a swarm of buzzing flies and saw a thin red column of dust in the distance, moving towards us like a twister. I had been mistaken; there was someone else out there. I was relieved to know it was our ride to town.

A few sweltering minutes later, a late-model Mitsubishi Triton covered in red dust pulled up. A guy dressed as if he had just finished shearing sheep hopped out, snatched up our ports, tossed them into the tray back, and without a word, climbed back behind the steering wheel. The window opened, and a voice from inside the canopy growled, "Shake the bloody flies off ya before you get in."

It was sound advice. I shook off the swarm of flies from my back and climbed into the air-conditioned cab. It was pure bliss. Bluey, as skinny as a rake and with a demeanour as tough as nails, wore a khaki army shirt with rolled-up sleeves, revealing his muscly ginger-haired forearms and freckled skin. Chewing on a matchstick as if it tasted good, he turned his steely blue eyes towards me from under an old, moth-eaten army diggers hat, and his stubbly face cracked into a partial grin.

"You or the other bloke, Axis Stone?" he asked slowly, with a drawl that would make any Texan green with envy.

"Did I stand out in the crowd at the airport?" I replied facetiously. "And who are you?"

"Bluey Wilson... odd-job-man for the pub," he muttered, the matchstick clenched between his teeth.

"That's Floyd, the pilot, on the back seat," I said. "So, we're an odd job then?"

"Yeah, guess so," he mumbled past the matchstick.

"I'm glad," I said, and that was about all the conversation I could muster. We had nothing in common. It was like trying to communicate with a toothbrush.

The rough, red dirt road tossed me around inside the cabin like I was riding a mechanical bull. Bluey seemed unfazed by it and made no effort to avoid the potholes. In fact, he seemed to hit every single one of them. It was a relief when we finally reached the bitumen.

As we drove into town, we passed a sign that read: "Shire population four hundred and sixty-nine." That probably explained Bluey's lack of social skills. He dropped us off at the front door of the single-story, pale yellow-painted pub, with its distinctive red guttering and grey corrugated iron roof. If you googled "outback pub," you'd probably find a picture of the Andamooka Opal Hotel. It was seriously iconic.

Floyd chuckled as Bluey drove off, "Ball of laughs, that bloke."

"Yep," I agreed. "Not the sharpest tool in the shed."

We checked in at reception, where a matronly-looking woman with a freckled face and ginger hair stood on the other side of the counter. She glared at me over her 1950s upswept cat's-eye glasses and, with a red painted smile that featured a gold tooth, courteously asked, "Got a booking, love?"

"You must be Mrs Wilson," I said, unsurprised. "We met your son."

"Yes, that was Bluey," she replied, her eyes enlarged twice their normal size by the thickness of her glasses.

"I could tell by the colour of his genes," I quipped.

My joke floated over her head like a waft of smoke. She then asked, "Your name, dear?"

Floyd got his own room, and we agreed to fly out at noon the next day. With only the name Josh Kovacs and a cell phone number he refused to answer as my lead, I went to my room, dropped off my port, slipped on my shoulder holster (minus the gun, as I couldn't travel with it), covered it with a light jacket, and checked myself in the bureau mirror. Satisfied with my appearance, I headed back to reception.

Mrs Wilson appeared after I rang the bell a couple of times. "Mrs Wilson, could you point me in the direction of Josh Kovacs' place?" I asked.

"You're in luck, Mr Stone. He just got back into town yesterday," she said slowly. "Last I saw, he was propping up the end of the bar." She gestured towards a doorway that presumably led to the bar. I thanked her with a nod and headed in that direction.

The bar was located at the back of the building, and the narrow corridor leading to it exuded a stale combination of beer, old carpet, furniture oil, and the mundane anonymity of countless worn-out lives. The small bar ran along the sidewall, with three empty round tables and chairs arranged in the centre of the room. A group of rough-looking men occupied the bar stools, being served by a surprisingly attractive young brunette bartender.

I took a seat at the bar and effortlessly caught her attention, although it wasn't a challenge since she was already eyeing me, much like everyone else in the room. The intense scrutiny made me feel as if I had just landed from outer space. I shot her a suave line accompanied by a cheeky smile, "Hi love, I'd kill for an ice-cold beer."

She raised an eyebrow, returning the interest, and replied, "Well, you won't have to kill anyone around here, love. I think I've got what you want." Her innuendo prompted me to raise an eyebrow in return. She poured me a Coopers draft beer and handed it over.

"Staying here?" she purred.

"Yeah, just overnight," I replied.

"On your ace?" she asked.

"I'd rather not be, but yeah," I said, packing as much innuendo into the sentence as possible.

Her long brunette hair was tied back in a ponytail. In her late twenties, a little rough around the edges, she possessed a rugged kind of beauty and displayed sharp wit. She wore a blue and white checked short-sleeve shirt, partially unbuttoned to reveal her cleavage, and a short denim skirt that accentuated her shapely legs. Leaning across the bar, I beckoned her closer with a finger, and we engaged in a confidential conversation.

"What's your name, honey?" I whispered.

"Rosita... And yours?" she whispered back, fluttering her long, black false eyelashes.

"Axis."

"Does that make you the centre of attention?" she quipped, smiling and revealing her pink tongue.

I signalled for her to come closer, and in a more covert manner, I continued, "Which one of these guys is Josh Kovacs?"

She nodded in the direction of a sombre-looking dude seated on a bar stool, hunched over his drink like a vulture. She then placed her hand on mine, a seductive gesture. I noticed a young, well-built guy with menacing eyes glaring at our hands, so I subtly withdrew mine. The glance I exchanged with Rosita conveyed my desire. Taking my beer, I made my way over to Kovacs.

As I approached him, I assessed his appearance: dark hair, 90s length, a triangular face with wide, expressionless eyes forming the base of the inverted triangle, a sharp-pointed nose, and a tight, thin mouth beneath it. He looked the kind of birddog who would lead his master into quicksand just for the hell of it. I guessed he was in his mid-fifties, but it was difficult to say for sure; he could be a smidgen younger. The beat-up look of someone down on their luck was unmistakable. He seemed so unaware that he didn't even notice my approach.

"Mr. Kovacs?" I inquired.

Head still lowered, staring into his empty glass as if he belonged inside it, he slowly looked up with impassive eyes. "Yeah, who's asking?" he muttered, his heavy Eastern European, possibly Polish, accent evident.

"The name's Axis Stone. We need to talk about something important."

"Not interested. Go away," he grumbled, returning his attention to his drained glass.

"Listen, pal," I snarled through gritted teeth, "either we find a table to have a chat, or I go to the cops and have you arrested... take your pick."

He hunched over like a crow on a branch, contemplating his options. He knew I meant business. Then, gradually, his tall, lanky figure rose from the bar stool like a giant bat. His glaring eyes narrowed with anger as he moved to a nearby empty table, pulling up a chair. I took a seat across from him, surveying the room. The décor and the wild-west-like patrons reminded me of a scene from the 1970s Hollywood classic movie "Blazing Saddles," just before the bar erupted into an all-out brawl. I hoped that scenario wouldn't unfold here.

"So, vat have you got to say zat's important enough to threaten me, huh?" he grumbled with his left eyelid twitching, which I took as an indication of unease.

I eyeballed him and growled without blinking, "Just two things... I want the deposit back you took for the opal you sold in L.A., and the name and address of the buyer who failed to kick the bin."

"Vot bloody opal? I sell plenty of stones, zat's my business."

"You know what I'm talking about... the Pride of Queensland. Read my lips Kovacs, I'm a private investigator representing Gary and Rod, do I need to say any more?"

"I don't care if you're representing ze president of ze United States," he snarled. "I don't have to give you ze time of day if I don't want to."

Now with a prominent tic under his left eye, he glared at me to emphasize his point. I knew I'd rattled his cage, so I calmly took a sip of my beer, slowly put the glass on the table, reclined in my chair, and stretched, allowing my shirt to open just wide enough for him to see my shoulder holster. I gave him plenty of time for it to register, then leaned with my elbows on the table and drilled him with a menacing glare.

"Listen good buddy, I don't have the same patience as Gary or Rod, so, if I were you, I'd cut the crap and deliver quick smart... I didn't come all this way for a beer."

By the look on his face, my stand-over tactics had worked. There was no way I wanted to involve cops, so there was a fair chunk of bluff in my diatribe.

"I don't carry zat sort of money with me, besides zere vere expenses," he groaned.

I was getting somewhere. Then, out of the corner of my eye, I caught Rosita pegging me and then noticed the young guy at the bar I'd seen earlier, turn his head to follow her eye-line to me. He shot me a serious stink-eye. Obviously, I was threatening his turf.

"I only have six grand left," Kovacs grumbled regaining my attention.

"Pull the other one!" I snapped.

"The deposit was only ten-grand," he pleaded with his arms held open piously.

"Ten-Gees US is nearly fourteen grand Australian, I told you not to bullshit me buddy and I mean it!" I growled.

"Okay, okay!" he stammered. "I got six thousand US cash left."

"Fine, I'll take it."

"It's in my safe, I can give it to you tomorrow."

I sank back in my chair, part one of the mission accomplished. "Cool, now fill me in on the botched deal," I snarled

"So, vat have you got to say zat's important enough to threaten me, huh?" he grumbled with his left eyelid twitching, which I took as an indication of unease.

I eyeballed him and growled without blinking, "Just two things... I want the deposit back you took for the opal you sold in L.A., and the name and address of the buyer who failed to kick the bin."

"Vot bloody opal? I sell plenty of stones, zat's my business."

"You know what I'm talking about... the Pride of Queensland. Read my lips Kovacs, I'm a private investigator representing Gary and Rod, do I need to say any more?"

"I don't care if you're representing ze president of ze United States," he snarled. "I don't have to give you ze time of day if I don't want to."

Now with a prominent tic under his left eye, he glared at me to emphasize his point. I knew I'd rattled his cage, so I calmly took a sip of my beer, slowly put the glass on the table, reclined in my chair, and stretched, allowing my shirt to open just wide enough for him to see my shoulder holster. I gave him plenty of time for it to register, then leaned with my elbows on the table and drilled him with a menacing glare.

"Listen good buddy, I don't have the same patience as Gary or Rod, so, if I were you, I'd cut the crap and deliver quick smart... I didn't come all this way for a beer."

By the look on his face, my stand-over tactics had worked. There was no way I wanted to involve cops, so there was a fair chunk of bluff in my diatribe.

"I don't carry zat sort of money with me, besides zere vere expenses," he groaned.

I was getting somewhere. Then, out of the corner of my eye, I caught Rosita pegging me and then noticed the young guy at the bar I'd seen earlier, turn his head to follow her eye-line to me. He shot me a serious stink-eye. Obviously, I was threatening his turf.

"I only have six grand left," Kovacs grumbled regaining my attention.

"Pull the other one!" I snapped.

"The deposit was only ten-grand," he pleaded with his arms held open piously.

"Ten-Gees US is nearly fourteen grand Australian, I told you not to bullshit me buddy and I mean it!" I growled.

"Okay, okay!" he stammered. "I got six thousand US cash left."

"Fine, I'll take it."

"It's in my safe, I can give it to you tomorrow."

I sank back in my chair, part one of the mission accomplished. "Cool, now fill me in on the botched deal," I snarled.

CHAPTER THREE

BY THE TIME Kovacs had finished explaining his tale of woe, we were the only customers left in the bar. He agreed to meet me back there at ten in the morning with the money, and then he left. I was confident it would happen; there was nowhere for him to run or hide. It was dark now, and I was hungry, so I called out, "Hello, anyone there?" from the bar.

After a couple of minutes, Rosita appeared, wearing a change of clothes and her hair out of the ponytail. She strode proudly towards the bar, looking stunning in a short-sleeved, floral A-line dress that fell to her knees. Her shiny brunette hair bounced on her shoulders, and she was indeed a sight for sore eyes.

"Sorry, Axis, I was out back changing," she said.

"Sad to have missed that," I quipped. "Hey, listen, I'm hungry, going anywhere tonight?"

"Is that a request for a date? What, in this excuse for a town?... Not likely, honey. You're already in the only place to go here."

"Okay, so what's a hot-looking gal like you doing in this dead-end joint like this?"

"Oh, that's a long story, my dear," she said coyly.

"I could be all ears and more over dinner?"

"Hmm, your place or mine?" she purred, with a seductive little smirk.

"Mine is limited to room service... so, um...?"

"Then mine it is. Come on, love, let's bail."

~ ~ ~

It was only a five-minute walk through the hot, dry night air to her pad; a small two-bedroom pad with the dining area, kitchen, and TV all in one. I commented, "Cosy little joint. You live alone?"

"No, with my big brother... he was the guy eyeballing you at the bar. Always out to protect little sister to the point of overkill," she said with a modicum of regret.

"So, where's big brother tonight?"

"Card night with his mates over at the White Dam. He won't stagger in until morning... blind drunk. Sit down, can I get you a drink?"

"Got any JD?" I questioned, taking a place on the three-seater lounge.

"Sure, how do you take it?"

"Uncontaminated over a couple of rocks, thanks."

She smiled smugly, and while she was in the kitchen making the drinks, I cased the place. Two plaques on the wall attracted my attention, both for boxing. I called out, "Your brother a prize fighter?"

"Yes... it was all happening for him until he got into trouble."

She cruised back, handed me a glass, then sat next to me.

"Cheers, big ears," she chuckled with the glass raised.

We touched glasses.

"A friend of mine used to say that," I said, remembering the lovely Lola. "So, what happened?"

"Ah, Vince was set for a title fight against the South Australian Middleweight Champion. One of his mates met him at the gym after training about a week before the big fight and asked him for a lift for him and his two buddies, home. On the way they stopped at a liquor store... the three of them got out and told Vince to wait in the car. They went into the shop and about ten minutes later, Vince heard gunshots. A cop car pulled up and arrested him, the others got away.

Vince had no idea he'd been set up as the driver for an armed robbery."

"Anyone hurt?"

"Yeah, the store attendant met his maker... and that's how we ended up here."

"What, after Vince had served time?"

"No, he got out on bail and we bailed alright, here to the dark side of the moon where nobody asks any questions."

"So, he's on the run from parole then? How long have you been here?"

"Only a month."

"Ah, so this is recent history then?"

"Yep, we've got no folks. I was freelance modelling but had to give it up and go with Vince or the cops would've made my life a misery. So, what brought Axis Stone to this place of desperados and crims?"

"To talk business with Josh Kovacs."

"Ha!" she chuckled macabrely. "Count your fingers after shaking hands with him, love," she warned. "He's a cheap-chiseller of the first degree. Everyone's after him for money. You in the opal game?"

I didn't really need to know that about Kovacs. Now I was worried he might do a bunk on me.

"No, I'm a private investigator."

She almost choked on her drink. "Shit, you're a cop!"

"Nar, not at all... don't worry, your little secret is safe with me."

"Phew, don't freak me out, love." She threw back her head, tilted the glass to her lips, and drank steadily until it was empty. Then she pushed the empty glass into my hand and purred, "Hold this, I can feel something coming off!"

She spun away from me, and her hands came up to her top. She spun faster as her fingers rippled down the line of buttons at the front of her dress like they were playing an arpeggio on a clarinet.

~ ~ ~

A while later, we were sitting at the dinner table. "Sorry it's frozen pizza," she smiled, a little embarrassed.

"I can think of something else I'd rather be eating," I said. I put down the slice of pizza and slid under the table. Then the sensuous moment was suddenly suspended by the sound of a door opening and the approach of heavy footsteps. I glanced around sharply from under the table at a pair of dirty work boots that had stopped there, and that was the last thing I remember because the lights went out.

~ ~ ~

I felt the back of my head... that explains the lump and the pounding headache. I figured I'd been walking in the desert for two hours and should be seeing signs of civilization by now. The vague tracks I was following had become clearer, possibly because I'd grown accustomed to looking for them. The heat of the relentless sun was beginning to sting my forearms and the tops of my shoulders. I couldn't work up a pee like the old Aboriginal had suggested, besides, I hadn't seen the plant with the little yellow flowers for ages. I knew if I didn't find water soon, I'd collapse in a heap, and that's when I came over a ridge and saw an old truck parked beside a windlass. It was an opal mine. I staggered over to it and yelled loudly down the square hole in the ground to get over the roar of the generator feeding power into it.

"Hello, is anyone down there?... Can you hear me?"

The electric windlass started up, and a man slowly emerged from the dark abyss, his foot in a loop at the end of a cable. He stepped out of the mine and brushed white powder off his face. His hat and clothes were covered in the talc-like stuff. He shook himself like a dog, and a great cloud of dust wafted into the dry air, got up my nose, and I sneezed, sending a plethora of flies off me into the air. He was staring at me like I'd just landed from Mars. Then, I remembered my face was blackened with sump oil, and I had a cloth on my head: what a sight.

"Sorry to get you up from your work," I said apologetically. "But I'm in a bit of strife, mate."

"I can bloody see that, mate... Hey, weren't you at the Opal Bar yesterday?" he rasped, with a three-pack-a-day voice.

"Yeah," I agreed, though I couldn't recollect seeing him there.

"I was only there a few minutes but remember you coming in and hooking up with shifty-old-Kovacs."

"Private investigator Axis Stone," I said, holding out my hand to shake. He took it with a vice-like grip, as hard as a rock with skin as rough as twenty-four grit sandpaper.

"Kevin Kent... so, what can I do for you, mate?"

"A sip of water would be good for starters, then maybe a lift to town if you've got time?"

"Axis old son, out here we've got nothing but bloody time," he drawled.

He fetched the water bag from the bull bar of his truck and handed it to me. I took a big swig, and it revived me somewhat.

"Let me lock up, and I'll run you into town. Don't drink too much water, it'll make you crook. When you're dehydrated, it's best to wait till you can get some electrolytes into ya, you know, Gatorade or one of them sports drinks," he advised assuredly.

After he'd locked down his mine, we climbed into his truck and motored off to town. I was surprised how far it was. I might not have made it if I hadn't found him. Along the way, I told him the story of the old Kokatha plainsman who'd rescued me and how he coaxed me to use the sump oil and to follow the car tracks.

He glanced at me from under his old weather-beaten army slouch hat with a doubting raised eyebrow on his unshaven face and growled, "Unlikely mate, I reckon it was a mirage. The Kokatha mob haven't been around here for well over fifty years, you'd be flat out finding one of them anywhere these days. They say radiation poisoning from the Pommy nuke tests in the '50s at Maralinga and Emu Field wiped them out over time... Nar mate, they're long gone."

I didn't argue the point. The whole episode had been as surreal as a Salvador Dali painting anyway.

"So, tell me about these blokes, firstly Vince the bartender's brother?"

"Vince, ha! He's trouble going somewhere to happen, that young bloke. He was there at the bar yesterday as well... had the evil eye on you, didn't he? Was it him who dumped you out in the never, never? Anyway, he got done down in Adelaide for armed robbery earlier this year and got off with a suspended sentence... they say he was the driver in a getaway car. Rumour has it his sister Rosita was working on the sly at one of them online sex sites where you pay for her to play, you know? Anyhow, it was run by some heavies and they decided to use what Rosita was doing to blackmail her brother into throwing a big fight that he had lined up... He's a professional boxer by trade, you know? Anyhow, they reckon the robbery was a fit-up coz he refused to throw the fight. After that, he needed to get out of town with Rosita because the heavies were after 'em for grassing to the cops... that's how he got the suspended sentence. A familiar story to you, I suppose?"

"Yeah, yeah, it happens a lot," I agreed, bumping my head on the turret—the dirt road was seriously potholed, but the rough ride didn't bother Kevin much, similar to Bluey. Must be a bush thing, I figured.

He went on. "Anyhow, Vince sees himself as Rosita's guardian. One time he heard talk she'd been with a feller out back at the Opal Bar. Well, he hunted that bloke down and gave him such a hiding he was lucky to live, they say. They flew the bloke to the hospital in Adelaide, and he never came back here. Since then, she's been on her best behaviour. I wouldn't like to get on the wrong side of him, he's got that killer look in them eyes."

None of what he had told me make me feel any better. Things just didn't seem to be going my way, and that made me hesitant to quiz him any further on Kovaks.

CHAPTER FOUR

I BIT THE bullet and eventually asked Kevin, "Tell me about Josh Kovacs?"

A sardonic smirk further creased his weather-beaten brow. "The shark? What more can I say? That about sez it all, don't it?"

As we pulled up outside the Opal Hotel, I took one last stab at it. "So, did he get the nickname Shark for actually ripping people off, or is that just a vicious rumour?"

He flicked up the brim of his hat with his finger and shot me a short, sharp telling glance. "Well, you know what it's like in a small town, mate," he sniggered. "Put it this way, a few blokes gave him stones on tick to take to the States and never saw 'em again... or the dough."

"How come he's still walking around then?" I asked.

"Ah well, that was a few years back... he disappeared after that. By the time he lobbed back, them particular blokes had moved on, as they do 'round here... but his dud reputation stayed with him. It's bloody tough enough trying to gouge a living out of the dirt without some bludger fleecing you of it once you score," he said, rolling a cigarette with one hand and then lighting it—something I hadn't seen done since I was a kid.

"Can I buy you a beer, Kev?"

"Next time, cobber... need to get back to gouging."

"Do you ever get to the big city?"

"Not if I can help it, all them people make me nervous."

Kevin was as tough as goat's knees—a top bloke—a real bush character. I shook his rock-like hand, hopped out of the truck, and watched it lumber off back towards his hole in the ground, in which he placed his trust that a strike would eventually fulfil his hopes and dreams.

~ ~ ~

After a serious scrub in a hot shower to cleanse myself of the stinking stew of sump oil and dust, I was feeling refreshed and hungry. Hoping breakfast was still on, I found the hotel café and sat down at a table by a window that looked out onto the main street, if you can call it that. The only company in the room was an elderly couple finishing up on breakfast. As I made my way past them to the buffet, they gave me a friendly good morning. I was half expecting to find Floyd the pilot there. I helped myself to bacon, eggs, toast, and a mug of hot coffee.

When I finished up and was getting set to leave, I sighted Kovacs through the window. He was on his way into the Opal Bar. Keeping his word restored a little of the faith I'd lost after talking with Kev. I was totally expecting him to bail on me. Breakfast was included with the room, so there was no charge. I ducked out to catch Kovacs at the bar.

~ ~ ~

He was in the same seat at the end of the bar as the day before, hunched over a drink like a giant predatory bird. He was the only customer. I pulled up a chair beside him. The bartender appeared.

"Hi, can you do a hot Bloody Mary?" I asked him, in need of the hair of the dog.

"Not often asked for here, mate... but I'll give it a shot," the middle-aged barman said jokingly, in a gruff voice.

"You're taking a risk asking for a mixed drink in zis joint," Kovacs growled into his near-empty glass like he had a bad cold.

"Yeah, well, risk-taking is part of my profession. I'm used to the disappointment if shit goes wrong. Speaking of that, I'm thrilled you're here."

"Why? You think I vas going to do a runner, hey?"

"Put it this way, I had my reservations."

"So do Indians," he joked. "You been listening to local rumours," he said with one eyebrow raised.

I was beginning to like the off-beat bloke. He plunged his hand belligerently into the side pocket of his jacket, produced an envelope, and slammed it down on the bar.

"Here, six gee's, give or take a hundred."

"What's this give or take business? There's either six grand or not!" I growled. Not prepared to accept his word, I opened the envelope and flicked through the US hundred-dollar bills.

"There's six thousand one hundred here?" I said, surprised.

"Like I said, give or take... I guess it was, give."

My drink arrived; it was in dire need of a haircut. "Lucky I didn't order a Harvey Wallbanger, this thing's got more vegetation than the Amazon jungle!" I complained to the bartender, with no rancour in my voice.

"Argh! It'll do you good, mate... jam-packed with vitamins," he chuckled.

Fighting my way through the forest in my glass, I peered through it at Kovacs. "Listen, I've been thinking about this deal, and you'll have to accompany me to the States. There's no point in me cold-calling this Hollywood producer cat of yours that didn't pay up; he'd probably just slam the door in my face. I know the type."

"He'll only do the same for me. Von't take my calls, nussing," he admitted, frustrated.

"Nussing?" I questioned.

"Nothing," he articulated, minus the accent. "Sometimes I get my worms mixed up."

I chuckled at his gag. "Why didn't you call the LAPD?"

"Because a few days after he'd given me the deposit, he handed over a credit note for me to bank here... I thought it vould be okay, but the bloody zing is still bouncing."

"Yeah well, that's illegal," I groaned, "same as a dud check."

"By then, it was all too hard. Okay, if you pay, I go with you, but I warn you, zere's no guarantee with zis bloody joker."

Kovacs was cracking me up. His strong accent gave his swearing even more impact.

"Right then, drink that down, go home, and pack a port. We leave for Adelaide at noon. Oh, one thing before you split, how did you smuggle the opal through customs?"

"Oh, zat's occupational hazard... if I had to pay duty each time I declare opals in every country, I'd go broke. Even if I take ze goods back out of ze country intact, for zem to pay you back ze duty, it takes bloody forever. So, I smuggle zem in, normally in my boots—I call it ze smuggler's hole, no-one ever checks inside your boots, especially if you've got stinky feet, ha! With ze Pride, I bought a brand-new pair of R.M Williams round-toed boots, two sizes too big for me. Ze stone fitted perfectly in ze toe of one boot, and I didn't even feel it ven I walk. Even ven I'm in ze hotel room, I leave valuables jammed in my boots with stinky socks—safe as bloody houses, mate," he grinned.

It was simple but effective: inventive stuff like that scores a big hit with me. "I'll remember that," I said. "Very clever... smuggler's hole, excellent."

~ ~ ~

I was confident it was the right move to take Kovacs with me to Hollywood. I rang Gary and told him; he agreed but warned me not to trust him. I recalled the warning to count my fingers after shaking hands with him—but I still had my fingers—that was at least positive.

I checked my watch. There was still an hour to kill before leaving for the airport, and there was something I needed to do, so I went for a stroll up the main street.

Scanning as I walked through the dry hot air, fighting off bush flies buzzing about my face, I saw what I was looking for on a dump beside a run-down old caravan parked on a vacant block. I collected the piece of four by two that was just the right length and sneaked down the side of Rosita's house up to the back door. It creaked open, and I slipped inside. It was quiet. Too early for them, they were obviously still in the sack. I tiptoed to the first bedroom door, holding the four by two at the ready. The door was slightly ajar. I peeked inside. Rosita was curled up sound asleep in bed. The next bedroom door, I figured, had to be Vince's. As I started up the short hallway, I heard the toilet flush. It had to be him. I moved quickly and waited by the bathroom door. As soon as he stepped out, I let him have it right across the back of the head as hard as I could hit. He went down like a lead balloon.

I stood over him. "Now we're square, buddy!"

One twitching eye squinted up at me. No way he was going to get up... he was down for the count.

~ ~ ~

A couple of days later, Kovacs and I checked into rooms at the Andaz Hotel on Sunset Boulevard. I stood at the window of my room and gazed in awe at the magical vista of Hollywood stretched out below. I'd never been to Hollywood before; it was like a dream come true—I could actually feel the pulsating buzz of showbiz in the air.

So far, it had been a pretty weird trip: since the pandemic, the population of the world had evolved into a species of faceless people, walking pairs of eyes peering out from behind surgical masks. In a way, it was the grand equaliser; the good looking and the not so good looking were now, for the first time, on an even keel. It also added a little intrigue to life, made a guy focus more on eyes, which in turn invoked a sense of mystery, in the same way it does when you see a woman wearing a Boshiya with only her exotic eastern eyes denuded.

Security checks at the airport on leaving were horrendous: they made us line up for two hours before check-in for an instant COVID test. If you'd had the mRNA editing jab and had a vaccine passport, you were ushered onto the meandering line A; if you hadn't, it was line B: a much shorter journey. I suspected those on the shorter journey were going nowhere. Passengers and crew were required to wear masks for the duration of the nineteen-hour direct flight. Then, upon arrival at LAX, another meandering line for another compulsory instant COVID test and then a line for a vaccine passport check. The Orwellian future had arrived. It was two hours before we got to customs, and a relief while standing at the baggage carousel to see an official digital sign declaring that masks were not mandatory in California.

The house phone rang, snapping me out of my revelry. It was Kovacs—he was ready to rock.

We met up in the lobby and then collected our Avis rent-a-car from the forecourt. Kovacs thought I was being extravagant, but I reckoned a guy hitting Tinsel-town for the first time needed the right wheels, and a red Mustang convertible perfectly fit the bill in my book. He grumbled that I was living in the wrong era, that I should've been a child of the '60s. He was beginning to notice my predilection for that epoch.

I climbed in behind the wheel and remembered the first law of driving on the right side of the road, or on either side of the road for that matter, is to always keep your passenger in the gutter. I drove out onto Sunset Boulevard and, after a few minutes, turned onto Laurel Canyon Drive. Our destination was Amor Road off Laurel Canyon, just before Mulholland Drive—the street made famous by David Lynch's 2001 film of the same name.

Nestled in a quiet wooded area on the side of the Hollywood Hills, blessed with a spectacular view of L.A., stood the stately two-story stucco mansion of film producer Carson Kincade. Unable to get him on the phone, we were left with no other option than a cold-call.

"Big house—plenty of bucks in this street," I said, pulling onto the sloping driveway.

"They call it the Producer's Row," Kovacs said.

There was a wide ochre-coloured raked-gravel driveway leading to the house. The small lawn had recently been given a manicure, but in reality, I wasn't sure if it was lawn or Astroturf. Most things in this town were supposedly fake. The double garage attached to the right side of the house was open, and I took note of the silver 718 Porsche Boxer parked beside a brand spanking new 911R. On my count, over three hundred grand tied up in two cars.

I parked out front of the imposing edifice before we ascended three steps onto the inlaid marble front porch. Kovacs pressed the doorbell, and muted chimes sounded from somewhere within. The noonday sun warmed my back as birds serenaded us from the trees. Moments later, the hefty door creaked open, revealing a middle-aged Asian maid clad in a neat black-and-white uniform. Kovacs greeted her as Dolly and inquired about Mr Kincade and Miss Diamond. She politely requested we wait and promptly closed the door. She reappeared moments later, ushering us inside. Trusting Kovacs' familiarity with the layout, she indicated that we should proceed to the swimming pool at the rear of the house.

Marble floors stretched beneath us, leading to a staircase spiralling up to a second floor. The place oozed affluence. Kovacs guided us down a narrow corridor lined with movie posters, all proudly displaying Carson Kincade's name in one capacity or another. Framed, posed photographs of Lexi Diamond, a Marilyn Monroe look-alike, added a glamorous touch. As we approached the end of the corridor, a montage of Hollywood's who's who, mainly from days gone by, adorned the walls.

Exiting through the expansive sliding glass doors onto a terrazzo patio, my gaze immediately fell upon a beauty lounging topless on a deckchair by the large, kidney-shaped pool. Her tanned, oiled body glistened in the midday sun.

Without acknowledging our presence, she asked in a husky voice, "So, Josh, what brings you back to Holly-weird?"

"Yes, Lexi, I'm back again. Zis time, with a friend. Meet Axis Stone."

Unfazed by a stranger's gaze on her scantily clad body, she sat up and nonchalantly covered herself with a white sarong. She then peered at me over the rim of her Bulgari Flora sunglasses, her eyebrow arched in curiosity.

"Hello, Miss Diamond. Your name truly does you justice," I remarked, rather pleased with my attempt at wit.

"Mr Stone... A man with class and an Aussie accent. First time here?" Her tone was languid.

"Yes, first time in Hollywood. It's refreshing to find the legends to be true."

"And what legend might that be, Mr Stone?" she inquired, her breathy voice hanging in the air as she gracefully slid her long, tanned legs off the deckchair and slipped her feet into a waiting pair of sandals.

"That the most beautiful women in the world are found here."

A sudden urge took hold of me, her tantalizing proximity proving irresistible.

"My, my, aren't we brimming with compliments? You'll go far in this town, Mr Stone." She extended a limp hand to shake.

As smooth as silk, her hand slipped into mine. "Please, call me Axis."

That single eyebrow rose above her sunglasses once more. She released my hand, reached for a gold case on a nearby table, and selected a cigarette. After lighting it, she took a deep drag, then exhaled a thin stream of smoke with an allure that contradicted the politically incorrect times. Don't get me started on political correctness. I've always been partial to the romance of yesteryear. Nowadays, it seems as though yesterday is forgotten far too quickly.

By my estimate, she was in her mid-twenties, untouched by Botox but likely enhanced by a few costly surgical procedures. Her nose, for instance, seemed a bit too perfect, possibly sculpted.

"We're here to see Carson," Josh interjected, snapping me out of my reverie.

With a slight increase in volume, she called, "Dolly?"

In an instant, Dolly reappeared. "Yes, Miss Diamond?" she asked, her strong Filipino accent easily recognisable.

"Is Mr. Kincade in his study?" Lexi inquired.

"Yes, ma'am," the young maid answered dutifully.

"Inform him that Mr Kovacs and his friend are here to see him."

"Yes, ma'am," Dolly repeated, then shuffled off.

Lexi removed her sunglasses, stood, and adjusted the sarong around her body. With curly shoulder-length platinum blonde hair, striking blue eyes, and a perfectly sculpted face accented by bright red lips, I could easily imagine her on the silver screen. She extinguished her cigarette in the ashtray before turning to lock eyes with me.

"You'll have to excuse me... I have a lunch meeting. Perhaps we'll meet again, Axis," she purred.

"If you happen to be around the Andaz Hotel at happy hour today, I'd like to buy you a drink and pick your brain about the ins and outs of this legendary town."

"You never know, Axis. You just never know," she responded with a feline grace, her smile as tantalising as her words.

Dolly reappeared and announced softly, "Mr Kincade will see you now."

My gaze lingered on the sensual sway of Lexi's hips as she vanished into the house.

"Remember what happened with Rosita?" Kovacs murmured slyly.

"Uh?"

"I'd tread carefully with Lexi, my friend. She's a notorious flirt. Your nemesis, Andamooka Vince, is nussing compared to Carson Kincade."

I got the drift and followed him back into the house towards the downstairs study.

CHAPTER FIVE

CARSON KINCADE WAS an arrogant son of a bitch, exactly as Kovacs had forewarned; the type of man who could easily turn on you. In his mid-fifties and looking every day of it, he was short, chunky, with receding grey hair that I was sure had been transplanted. Sporting a large bulbous nose and bags under his muddy-brown eyes that could pack enough gear for a dirty weekend, his wrinkled round face displayed all the signs of far too many excesses. His lips were set tight in a permanent scowl. A leaf-green silk shirt, unbuttoned at the front, gave him the look of a character straight off the album cover of the Bee Gees' Nights on Broadway, and the chunky gold chains around his neck and wrist bore testament to that. He was the kind of guy you disliked at first sight. The walls of his study were adorned with self-indulgent memorabilia, award citations, film crew photographs, shots of him with movie stars and famous directors, and a couple of gold records. A photo of him with Alfred Hitchcock was particularly impressive. If I didn't know any better, I would have assumed we were in the man cave of a self-appointed Mr Hollywood.

Ensconced in a large black leather chair behind an antique mahogany desk, Kincade glared at us through thick eyeglasses and then growled with the three pack-a-day timbre of an ex-radio DJ.

"So, to what do I owe the pleasure this time, Kovacs?"

"You've been hiding from me Carson … not taking my calls and zat has caused me serious grief. Your credit note bounced all over

Australia, left me with ze egg on ze face and cost me plenty," Kovacs growled, visibly annoyed.

Kincade's expression soured his already sullen face. His rich fake-tanned complexion started to mottle.

"Shit happens, Kovacs!" he growled. "Especially in my business … so, who's your friend, a heavy or something?" His chuckle was more of a guffaw.

Feeling about as welcome as a fart in an elevator, I said, "Axis Stone, private detective," and extended my hand, which he chose to ignore.

"Way out of your jurisdiction by the accent," he sneered.

We were standing around aimlessly, so I pulled up a chair and sat. Kovacs followed suit.

I levelled my gaze at him. "Look Kincade, we're not here to stir up trouble, but the owners of The Pride have a right to know when they'll get their money, and you have a moral obligation to tell them."

His expression softened slightly. "Of course, you're right, Stone … I apologise if I appeared to be hiding from you Kovacs but once I've explained the situation, I'm sure you and Stone will understand."

It was a greasy response. Josh was about to retort when I motioned for him to wait and hear the man out.

"Go ahead Mr Kincade," I said, managing to keep my tone cordial.

"Okay, when I met you four months ago, Kovacs, it was like you were an angel. I don't have to tell you that my best years as a film producer are behind me, and good scripts have dried up coming my way a while back. So, when I was offered to invest in a film with a great script and big-name actors attached, I jumped at it. To buy in would cost all my cash and stock reserves plus a mortgage on this house. We're talking five million bucks here. It was all above board until just before I met you at the Gerry Mansfield party. In case you don't know him Stone, Gerry Mansfield is a film investment wheel here in Hollywood. Anyway, I'd been told another two hundred grand was needed from me to fund additional script development, and if I couldn't pay up, I'd have to take a back seat in the production instead of getting an up-front executive producer credit. You have to understand that here in Hollywood, you're only as good as your last film. My use-by-date was nearly up ... I needed this deal to stay in the mix. So, when you offered me the opal, I saw an opportunity. I could give them the stone, give you a credit note to buy myself ninety days, and within that time, the full budget of the film would be raised, and I'd get the two hundred grand plus some of my investment back."

"What's the full budget?" I asked.

"A hundred and twenty million dollars."

"Holy mackerel, zat's a lot of money!" Kovacs exclaimed.

"Not for a film like this with bankable assets like Margot Robbie and Jamie Dornan attached."

"So, are they signed up?" I queried.

"Not yet, but they've read the script and want some small changes, well at least their agent does ... that's why the rewrite ... it's all normal."

"So, you expect me to tell my client zat he is now an investor in a Hollywood movie?" Kovacs snarled.

"No, no, no... just give me until the end of the month, that's all I'm asking," he pleaded. "Look, they took the stone as collateral and still have it. If by the end of the month," he glanced at the calendar on his desk, "in two weeks the deal's not done... worst case scenario is you'll get the stone back and you can keep the deposit."

A pregnant pause filled the room as I considered his proposition. "Alright, alright, but I'll need a few things to facilitate that arrangement," I insisted. "First, I'll need a letter of intent from the production company outlining your involvement and the numbers... plus the letter will acknowledge the payback and the timing of it. Second, I want evidence they have the stone, and third, I want a notarised agreement from you outlining what you've just proposed."

"And when do you want all this by?" he snarled, his body language suggesting he found my demands exasperating.

"The sooner the better, it's costing us money to be here," I said, maintaining eye contact with him.

Kovacs' face was a mask of discontent. There was a pause as Kincade mulled over our demands.

"Okay, okay, agreed," he spat irritably. "I'll talk to my attorney, try and have it for you... umm, in a couple of days."

"I want a lien over ze two Porsches in ze garage," Kovacs growled. "I don't trust you, Kincade, not after ze run-around you've given me."

Kincade scoffed, "Ha! That'd be no use to you. I don't own the damn things; they're both leased. Man, get it into your head, this is America, no-one owns goddamn anything here."

"You've got to have something we can hold in escrow as security, jewellery, bonds, deeds... something?" Kovacs demanded.

Kincade let out a cynical snigger. "There's nothing left, you'll just have to take my word for it."

"Your word's not worth ze paper it's written on. I mean it!" Kovacs snapped, jumping to his feet aggressively.

Kincade flinched.

I didn't want to inflame the situation. It was clear Kovacs didn't trust the deal, but I was prepared to go along with it. There was really no other option. I needed to calm Kovacs down. "My friend here has a point, Kincade. Put yourself in his place. After the embarrassment he suffered with his client, it's understandable he's reluctant to trust you."

Kincade stood to terminate the meeting. He was even shorter than I had first assumed.

"Let me have a word with my wife when she comes home... the jewellery is hers, it would be her call," he snarled without conviction.

"Alright, call me tonight at the Andaz Hotel, room 617," Kovacs snapped impatiently. "We'll see ourselves out," he closed, scorn dripping from his words.

~ ~ ~

Kovacs sat in silence with a sour expression on his face as we drove the Mustang back down Laurel Canyon to Sunset. The sight of giant billboards — iconic symbols of Hollywood — dotted along both sides of the boulevard gave me a thrill. Up in the hills, I could see the iconic Hollywood sign towering over the city: an enormous reminder that we were in the land of magic. I was utterly captivated.

Eventually, Kovacs broke his silence. "I don't trust him. He'd say anysink to get rid of us."

"You don't think he'll do what he said?" I asked evenly.

"Nah, it vuz just a pile of bullshits. You've got to remember, I vuz at the party and I heard nussing about him being attached to a movie. Zis is Hollywood, bullshits is a way of life here, zey even have zere own word for it... blag... Kincade or his lush wife mentioned nussing, not a word about a movie... zat tells me he's full of crap."

"So, he has no intention of paying for the opal, he's just trying to scam us?"

"I believe so. Maybe he's buying time... Argh, who knows?" he dismissed, grumbling.

"How did you get an invite to such a fancy party?"

"A friend of mine is ze head jeweller at Kazan Jewels in Beverly Hills. I showed him ze Pride but zay weren't in the market for such a large boulder opal. He had an invite to ze party zat evening, so he invited me to tag along."

"Was the Pride too expensive for them?"

"No, ze opal business is like zat," he said, sounding dispirited. "You just have to be lucky when you're offering an important stone to industry types. On ze rare occasion, it's something zay are looking for, but mostly because opals are semi-precious, zay prefer to spend their money on more valuable gems like diamonds which have a more definite resale price. So, zay only look for an opal when a customer specifically requests one."

"Right, so a customer would ask them for an opal and they'd go hunt one down?"

"Yes, it's ze birthstone for October, so generally it's ven a high-roller is looking to buy a birthday present for his wife or girlfriend, or something like dat."

"Why aren't they as important as diamonds and so forth?"

"Opals are just as rare, in fact rarer … zay formed only once sixty-million years ago, and only in certain parts of ze world, especially Australia. But zay don't have ze investment resale value diamonds or emeralds have. Zay're semi-precious, whereas diamonds and such are considered precious."

"They can crack, can't they?"

"From some areas, yes maybe, but zis is most unlikely — zat's just bad press."

"Why is The Pride so special?"

"Is a big stone... harlequin pattern Queensland black boulder opal, stunning, and extremely rare."

"Harlequin, what does that mean?" I asked.

"Red and green checkerboard pattern. The Pride is ze only one of its kind."

We arrived at the Andaz Hotel. I handed the car over to the valet and we headed to our rooms. In the elevator, I asked Kovacs to call his friend at Kazan Jewels to get Gerry Mansfield's number: it would be worth contacting him to get his personal opinion of Kincade and his supposed movie deal.

~ ~ ~

It was a sweltering summer day, and I had worked up quite a sweat. The rooftop sundeck with its inviting pool and refreshments beckoned. However, purchasing a SIM card for my GSM phone remained on my to-do list, given that U.S. networks primarily used CDMA. That would have to wait, though.

As I prepared to leave my room, draped in a white robe with a towel slung over my shoulder, the room phone interrupted my departure. Picking up the receiver, I was greeted by the sultry voice of Lexi Diamond, who informed me she was nearby and wanted to take me up on my offer for a happy hour drink. I suggested she join me on the rooftop for a late lunch instead.

The rooftop view was awe-inspiring, and I'm not talking about the sprawling L.A. cityscape. Three sunbathing beauties — a blonde, a brunette, and a redhead, the ultimate trifecta — were the true spectacle. Each woman, independent of the others, seemed to be open for conversation, each flashing me inviting smiles. I felt as if I'd stumbled into paradise.

Stripping off my robe, I flashed my most charming grin at the trio and plunged into the cool pool water with an Olympic-grade dive. Emerging after a few invigorating laps, I found only the brunette remaining. As she nonchalantly applied oil to her bronzed legs and peeked at me over her sunglasses, I decided to put an end to the flirtation. He had me fooled from a distance indeed. Sitting at a shaded table, I reminded myself that things in Hollywood weren't always as they appeared — some women weren't women.

Just as I was about to summon the attendant for a drink, a striking woman appeared at the entrance. Lexi, dressed to kill, made the previous blonde and redhead seem ordinary.

She sauntered towards me and greeted me in a sultry voice, "Well hello, Axis Stone, fancy meeting you here."

Rising from my chair, I gestured for her to sit. We both removed our sunglasses, and I called over the attendant. Lexi was decked out in a black mini dress, paired with black, ankle-strap high heels that I estimated cost her a small fortune.

"Dig the shoes," I complimented.

With her legs crossed, she slipped off one of her shoes. "I just bought them at Bloomingdale's in the Beverly Center. They're SJP's."

"Expensive?" I asked, subtly appreciating her vivid red pedicure.

"Just under six hundred. I love shoes," she confessed, gently massaging her bare foot. "But they always hurt the first time you wear them."

"Let's order some food. Looking at your feet has made me hungry," I joked. A foot fetish can be a perplexing thing at times. She caught my drift and raised an eyebrow in curiosity.

CHAPTER SIX

WE HAD FINISHED our meal, and I decided it was time to delve deeper. "So, Carson claims he's close to landing a major movie deal, his first in a while?"

Lexi leaned back in her chair, donning her sunglasses before taking a sip of her iced chai latte. "Yeah, well, I'm not exactly holding my breath," she replied, her tone edged with cynicism.

"Do I detect a hint of pessimism? You don't believe it'll happen?"

"Been there, done that... This isn't the first time, honey. He's only trying to keep me around."

"Really? High maintenance, are you?" I prodded.

"It's not about money, honey..." she waxed lyrically.

Immediately, my mind raced to the possibility of unmet needs in the bedroom. But catching the look in my eye, she clarified, "It's about my acting career."

"Ah, I see," I understood. "You're expecting a part in the movie?"

"Like I said, he's promised me parts before. That's how we got together. Four years ago, he still had clout. He cast me in a leading role for a film that was supposed to be my big break. But it fell through at the last minute."

"That's unfortunate."

"Yeah, I later found out it was all pillow talk. It was never going to happen," she spat, her bitterness evident. "You know how long it takes a naïve twenty-year-old from Milwaukee to learn the ropes here? Especially how to see through all the BS. Everyone's in the movies – the busboy, the taxi driver. Everyone has a story about their upcoming or missed out film project. Every paunch-bellied, cigar-smoking old man uses a movie role to entice young girls like me to... cater to his needs. This town is built on stories, Axis. It's all a façade. The gutters are filled with the dreams of the naïve."

I remembered a song by an Aussie band, Two-Up, called Hollywood. I shared the lyrics: "Scripted hopes displayed on sunset, pawnshops carry tales of hard-knocks, you can break a leg, when you're climbing up to the screen... in Hollywood."

A knowing smirk crossed her face. "So true. Whoever wrote that obviously knew this place."

"I guess so. It seems like you might have a little black book of interest-bearing grudges, Lexi?" I teased.

"Sure do... and it's quite a read," she retorted, her tone still biting.

"So, do you think Carson's new flick will get financed?"

"Firstly, it's not his. Secondly, it'll happen with or without him. But right now, he doesn't have the capital to play. It's a great script, and I intend to be part of it. There's a role just for me."

"But he's already invested five million, including the opal."

"The opal, ha! That's a joke. He bought it from Josh Kovacs, hoping it'd serve as collateral. Kovacs claimed it was worth a quarter mil, but the brokers in Vegas valued it at less than half that."

"That's surprising. Why?"

"Because that's how they value anything other than property or cash."

"Wait, let me get this straight. A mob in Vegas owns the script?"

"Yes."

"And they're using it to raise funds?"

"Exactly, like selling shares. The more you invest, the more influence you have in the production. Noticed the long list of executive producers in opening credits these days?"

"That makes sense. Influence over things such as say casting?"

"Yep."

"How much are they raising?"

"They only raise ten percent of the budget, to finalise the script and attract big names."

"Then?"

"They secure a top director and pitch it to financiers, underwriters, networks, and studios."

"And if no one bites?"

"Initial investors lose. But if it flies, they get their investment back plus a decent chunk of the film."

"Quite a gamble. No wonder these dudes are from Vegas." I leaned back in my chair, adding, "Kovacs brought me in to possibly finance Carson so he could pay for the opal."

"Wait, Carson didn't pay for the opal?"

"Exactly."

She looked genuinely shocked, and I could see her processing this revelation. She was silent for a moment before declaring, "I need a drink. Something stronger."

I called over the attendant and ordered a couple of JDs on the rocks. Lexi removed her sunglasses, her eyes meeting mine with a newfound intensity.

"Look, they needed a quarter of a mil for script amendments," she began. "Carson saw it as an opportunity to push his case for a majority shareholding and pitched it to them. They agreed but wanted cash. Carson got us an invite to a party at the Hollywood mansion of attorney and film finance mogul Gerry Mansfield, thinking he'd be able to cut a deal with Gerry for the quarter of a mil. But Mansfield didn't want to know about Carson, he figured he was past his prime but he sure wanted to know about me. That's when Carson met Kovacs and the opal deal came up. Kovacs agreed to take a ten-grand deposit, then a credit note for the stone. He figured he could close the deal for the film by only spending ten grand, the bank would pay out on the credit note — obviously, they didn't. So, that's how the deal got done but Carson didn't expect Al to value the opal at only a hundred grand."

"Why only a hundred?" I pressed.

"That's how much they could unload it for in a hurry. They needed cash. Trouble is Carson is causing waves and Al wants him out, he finally realised Carson is old hat."

The drinks arrived.

"You said Al, who's that?"

"I really don't know why I'm telling you all this, Axis," she admitted sheepishly.

"Because I'm such a nice guy," I quipped.

She raised that sexy single eyebrow at me again.

"Al Head owns Outlaw Productions, they own the property and let me tell you ... he's the sort of guy you don't wanna mess with."

"What, he's a gangster or something?"

"Well, let's just say he's not the sort of guy to get on the wrong side of ... I warned Carson to quit his antics but he's too pigheaded ... doesn't listen — especially to a woman — thinks all women are stupid and only good for one thing."

"Hmm, I know the type. How do you know Outlaw isn't just conning Carson out of his bread?"

"You gotta go by the script. The trouble with Outlaw is they're not from here and this is their first picture. But Carson has to take what he can get, so—"

"Where does that leave it?"

She paused to think. "I guess Carson still owes them the difference; a hundred and fifty grand."

"And if he doesn't pay up, what happens then to you and him?"

"He misses out on a majority share and I have to find some other way of getting the part."

"Gerry Mansfield or Al Head?"

"One or the other or both," she said with a wry smile. "I've known Al a while. I introduced him to Carson in the first place. Anyhow mister Stone, what do you hope to gain from all of this?" She said with a sexy, smug look.

"Maybe to jump the line ahead of Gerry and Al," I said suggestively.

"Oh really! So, what's on offer then?" she purred, licking her crimson voluptuous lips.

I leaned across the table, lifted her sunglasses, and peered into her azure-blue, almond-shaped eyes.

"Dessert?" I said smoothly.

A wicked gleam lit up her eyes, and her lips parted into a cheeky smile.

~ ~ ~

Ten minutes later we were in my room. Soon as we got inside the door I took her in my arms. I could feel her body soft and pliant against my own. Her lips returned the pressure of mine, and our tongues met briefly.

Sometime later, I gave her a gentle kiss on the lips and closed the door behind her. The timing was perfect; the phone rang. It was Kovacs.

"Hey Josh what's news?"

"I got you a SIM from Seven Eleven."

"Thanks. Did you get hold of Mansfield?"

"Yes, I called him but it vasn't very pleasant. Let's meet in ze bar and talk about it, it's happy hour."

I thought happy hour was over for me but agreed to meet him downstairs in fifteen minutes — time enough to freshen up and change.

~ ~ ~

The Riot Bar on the ground floor was packed to the rafters with the cool set — it is, after all, one of the trendiest places to be seen in West Hollywood.

I spotted Kovacs in the corner of the room, holding a small table for us where the in-house music wouldn't be too intrusive. When I sat down, he handed me a drink.

"Cheers," he said.

"Yeah, here's to a successful trip," I countered.

"Give me your phone."

I handed it over and watched him change the SIM. He handed me a small card.

"This is your new number."

"Thanks, man. What do I owe you?"

"Nussing, it cost little and I had little."

I liked Kovacs; his oddball dry sense of humour was becoming.

"So, what did our Mr Mansfield have to say?"

"Not impressive, my friend… at ze mention of Kincade, he almost hung up in my ear."

"Dead-set. Our boy doesn't seem to be winning the Hollywood popularity stakes, does he?"

"I'd say zat vud be ze understatement of ze year. Anyhow, I managed to talk him round somewhat, and he told me zat as a filmmaker, Kincade is a has-been, not bankable… and zat's a death sentence for a producer in Hollywood. I asked him about some new production Kincade vas mooted as being involved in, and he gave an emphatic no to anything on ze cards to be produced here."

"So, if it's a production from another place, it might well be true?"

"Yes, I suppose so."

I filled him in on what I'd learned from Lexi, omitting the mischief I'd got up to with her in my room.

CHAPTER SEVEN

T
HE HOUSE PHONE woke me halfway through the night. It was a distress call from Lexi. She was locked in a room at the house, fearing for her life after a terrible fight with Kincade. She had told him she was leaving him, and he had exploded in anger. I urged her to call the police, but she didn't want to attract attention. Against my better judgment and in defiance of the PI credo to never get involved in domestic disputes, I gave in to her pleading and committed to go to her aid. The little head had overruled the big head.

I decided not to call Kovacs and went alone to the Kincade residence.

~ ~ ~

I left the car in the driveway and approached the front door. It was wide open. I glanced around and noticed that the lights were on in the house opposite, which struck me as odd for that time of night. I stepped inside. The place was lit-up like Christmas, and a shattered vase on the floor in the lobby indicated a violent struggle. For some reason, I felt drawn to Kincade's study at the end of the hallway.

I entered the study. Carson Kincade lay on the floor, a look of permanent surprise on his face. He was dressed only in undershorts. The pool of blood around his head and the position of his body suggested he had been shot execution style: shot at close range. It was a crime scene, and I was in a foreign country—I needed to get out of there quickly. I scanned the room for any clues. Signs of a struggle and a bloody letter opener on the floor indicated that Kincade might have fought back, but there was nothing else of significance. As I started to head back to the hallway, I was suddenly blinded by a bright light, accompanied by furious shouting.

"Police! Get on the floor with your hands behind your head, now!"

I complied, hitting the floor as ordered. I had seen enough American reality shows to know what happens if you don't obey the police here. In a matter of seconds, it seemed like a hundred heavily armed cops stormed into the place, yelling frantically. It was utter chaos.

I was roughly patted down, handcuffed, read my rights, dragged outside, shoved into the back of a police car, and driven to a police station.

In no time at all, I had gone from a comfortable bed at the Andaz Hotel to a holding cell at the Beverly Hills PD on Rexford Drive.

~ ~ ~

The words "Beverly Hills" evoke thoughts of class and style, but let me tell you, as soon as you add the acronym "PD," that notion disappears faster than a politician's promise on Election Day.

I sat on the edge of a bunk in my cell, my face in my hands, for what felt like hours before I was finally taken to an interrogation room.

A middle-aged man dressed in a beige suit with a fancy silver and turquoise Hopi Indian bolo slide around his pale-yellow shirt entered a moment later. He appraised me as if I were up for auction, pulled up a chair across from me, and placed an iPad on the table between us. His face was pleasant enough, sporting a full salt and pepper moustache and matching haircut, albeit with sideburns longer than currently fashionable. He was a caricature of a Latino cowboy. As he spoke, I expected a different accent, and I wasn't disappointed—it was the gravelly voice of a man who had been a heavy smoker for most of his life.

"Detective Chuck Santana... You've identified yourself as Axis Stone from Sydney, Australia, is that correct?"

"Yes, it is, Detective."

"What is your profession, Mr Stone?"

"I'm a private detective."

"I see... Why are you in Los Angeles?"

"I'm on a case."

"I didn't get out of bed at goddamned five in the morning to do a cryptic crossword... Elaborate, son," he growled.

Taking the hint, I explained the case without divulging anything about the opal, the identity of my client, or any other names except for Kovacs. He jotted down notes on his iPad and sent a message as soon as I mentioned where Kovacs and I were staying. I anticipated that it wouldn't be long before they picked up Josh and brought him in to corroborate my story.

"Can I ask you a question, Detective?"

"Why not?" he sighed tiredly. "I'm done asking any."

"Was Mr Kincade's partner, Lexi Diamond, at the house when the police arrived?"

"No, the only living person in that house was you, which is why you're here visiting us."

"Were you at the crime scene?"

"No, Lieutenant Williams from Organised Crime took care of that."

"So, did he report a bloody letter opener on the floor next to the body?"

"No. But that doesn't mean it isn't in evidence. Where are you going with this?"

"I suspect Kincade might have wounded his killer. Am I under arrest on suspicion of murder?"

"No. You weren't carrying the murder weapon. You're being held until we can clear you. Look, you must be familiar with murder investigations; you know the damn drill."

"I can provide you with a senior contact at the New South Wales Police Department to verify my credentials if that would help."

"No, that won't be necessary."

"You mentioned Lieutenant Williams from Organised Crime... Does that mean Kincade was under his watch?"

"You know I can't answer that, Stone," he said dismissively.

I was taken back to the cell. After about an hour, a uniformed officer came and escorted me upstairs to Chuck Santana's office. He was in conversation with Kovacs. The uniformed officer left me there, and Santana gestured for me to sit. I glanced at Kovacs, shaking my head in a doleful manner.

"Mr Kovacs has confirmed your story, Stone. However, I have a few questions that need clarification before I can release you. You said Lexi Diamond called you to say she was having a fight with Kincade and that she was afraid. Why didn't you tell her to call the police?"

"I did, but she said she didn't want to attract undue attention—something I expect would be common when dealing with showbiz folks in this town."

"Definitely. But why did she call you rather than someone else? As I understand it, she'd only just met you," he said casually.

It wasn't difficult to tell that he was a clever cop—the question was loaded.

"Maybe she likes me. Who knows?"

"Does she know you're a PI?"

"No, I told her I'm in film finance... keeping the cards close to my chest. Do you think she did him?" I asked.

"Two bullets point-blank in the back of the head tells me no."

"Just a budding actress from Milwaukee," I said forlornly.

"Milwaukee, you say?" Santana sat forward in his chair and checked the file in front of him. "I have her from Vegas?"

"Like I always say, never believe vat a woman tells you," Kovacs cackled under his breath.

"Wait a minute, that's where she said Outlaw Productions is located," I added.

"What does Outlaw Productions have to do with this?" Santana growled. "Get it into your head, Stone, this is a murder investigation, withholding evidence is a felony."

There was a sharp knock at the door.

"Come on in, Lieutenant," Santana loudly invited.

One look at the guy who entered, and I immediately recognised trouble. He was the type of bloke you wouldn't leave alone with your kids. Tall and thin with a rat-like face and beady eyes; he reminded me of a praying mantis.

Santana gestured at me. "Axis Stone is an Australian PI, and Kovacs here is his assistant. This is Slim Williams, now I know that sounds like I'm introducing a country and western singer, but I assure you he's a lieutenant."

The lieutenant's sullen, chiselled face didn't crack at the light-hearted gag. In fact, he hardly even acknowledged our presence. He simply lowered himself into a chair and sat there hunched, resembling a vulture perched on a branch, waiting for its turn at a roadkill carcass.

"I explained before, Slim was in charge of the crime scene, so if you have any questions about it, Stone, he's your man. He'll do his best to answer, won't you, Lieutenant?"

Without changing his morose expression, Williams offered an ever-so-slight nod.

"Yes, I have a couple of queries. I found Kincade because of a distress call I received from his partner, Lexi Diamond. I didn't have much time at the crime scene, but I saw signs of a struggle and no sign of Miss Diamond. Any clues as to where she might be?"

"No," Williams replied expressionlessly.

He made it clear that he had no intention of discussing the case with me. I pressed on regardless.

"Right... So, did you find a bloody letter opener on the floor in Kincade's study, next to the body?"

"No."

The guy wasn't going to cooperate at all, but I persisted. "What do you think happened?"

"He was murdered," he growled bluntly.

I glanced at Santana. "Is this bloke always so obliging, or doesn't he like my aftershave?"

Williams reacted. "Look, I don't know what they do in Austria—"

I cut him off, growling facetiously, "That's Australia, mate... a little further south."

"Until I get forensics and a med report, I'm not about to discuss it with anyone. It might still be suicide," Williams grumbled.

"Vas zere a note?" Kovacs queried.

"I think the two bullet holes in the back of his head might rule out suicide, unless Kincade was an extraordinary shot," I growled with utmost cynicism.

"I don't have to take this from some foreign private dick. Will that be all, Detective?" Williams snarled and then clambered to his feet.

Santana got the message. There was no love lost between us, so he concluded the meeting. Without saying another word, Williams stalked out of the room.

"Ball of laughs, that bloke. Personality of an armpit," I scoffed, and Kovacs chuckled.

"Ah, don't mind him. We call him the undertaker around here. No sense of humour. He's only been at this office three months, transferred from Vegas. It'll take him a while to get used to the way we do things here. You're staying up on Sunset, so give me the day, and we'll catch up tomorrow for breakfast at Denny's... say 9 a.m. Can you do that?" Santana asked pleasantly. We nodded. "You know Denny's? It's a diner on Sunset, just down from your hotel... I'd meet you at the Riot House, but I'm likely to see too many ex-cons I'd know," he sniggered.

"I know vere Denny's is," Kovacs confirmed.

Santana handed me his calling card. "Here, in the meantime, if you hear from Miss Diamond, tell her she needs to give me a call."

We stood up.

"Do we have any reason to be concerned for our safety?" I asked, prompted by his comment about gangsters at our hotel.

"Yes, until I talk to Miss Diamond, we must assume that what you told me is connected to the murder."

"It's not looking good," Kovacs mumbled dispiritedly.

"Lay low for now," he advised. "I'll know more by tomorrow, and you can plan what you need to do from there. For now, I don't advise saying anything to anyone."

We shook hands. He had a good firm handshake.

"Much obliged for being upfront, Detective Santana," I said genuinely.

"Call me Chuck or Carlos. I don't mind which," he thundered with a copacetic smile.

Carlos had a patrol car drop us back at the hotel. It had been a long night, and I was still seething over Williams' obnoxious attitude. Kovacs suggested having breakfast by the pool to lighten the mood, and I didn't need my arm twisted to comply.

~ ~ ~

It was a little disappointing. It was too early for any eye-candy at poolside, but at least we had the place to ourselves. A few laps in the pool refreshed me and dispelled any ill feelings I had been harbouring. We downed a few coffees to get the vibe up, and I was beginning to feel better when the pool attendant brought over a cordless phone. I recognised Lexi's dulcet tones at the other end and covered the mouthpiece to whisper covertly to Kovacs, "Lexi."

"Give her Santana's number," he reminded me.

With one hand, I fumbled for Santana's calling card in my wallet and then pressed the speaker button so Kovacs could hear.

"I'm in trouble, Axis... you've got to help me," she pleaded.

"It's a murder investigation, Lexi. I can't help you. I'm only a film financier..." I lied.

"I didn't kill him, Axis... after I called you... I... I heard shots... I went downstairs. I thought he'd shot himself, but then I saw someone run out of the house and get into a car with the engine running."

"Are you saying it was a hit?"

"I don't know. All I could think of was to get out of there. I'm sorry if it put you in an awkward position."

"I wouldn't exactly call spending the night in jail and being interrogated by cops 'awkward,'" I growled.

"Oh, I'm so sorry, Axis... I... I," she whimpered.

"Look, you have to call Detective Santana ASAP. I'll give you—"

"No!" She abruptly cut me off. "Can't trust the cops," she snarled adamantly.

"Where are you now?"

"At a friend's place. She's an actress."

"Who would have wanted Kincade dead?"

"Plenty of people."

"Why?"

"He made lots of enemies over the years. You're asking too many questions, Axis," she snapped irritably.

"What about this mob you told me about... Outlaw Productions... Al Head?"

"That's a movie deal—"

"Yes, but Carson owes them buckets of money?"

"He does, I mean, did... but they wouldn't... look, I've... I've got to go," she said nervously.

"We should meet up."

"I'll call you later," she added hurriedly.

I gave her my new cell phone number, handed the phone back to the attendant, and squinted through the glaring sunlight at Kovacs sitting opposite me. "Something's not right with her," I summarised the call.

"Is she suspicious of your cover story... or is it because she won't talk to ze cops, or something else?"

"She can't stay on the run from the law. They'll put an APB out on her, and she'll wind up in even more trouble. I need to convince her to talk to Santana. But there's something in her voice that just doesn't ring true. As soon as I mentioned Outlaw and Al Head, she clammed up."

"I noticed you didn't mention Al Head to Santana. Why not?"

"Because we still need to complete our mission, and we won't get anywhere with the cops breathing down our necks... You didn't say anything to Santana about the opal, did you?"

"No, now vey, it's here illegally. Ve have to keep it hush-hush. Maybe ve should focus on Al Head and Outlaw Productions?"

"You read my mind, buddy. And I think Lexi is the key."

"Vere is she?"

"She said she's staying with an actress friend."

"I might be able to get us a lead if I try Gerry Mansfield again."

"No," I said, "I've got a better idea. And if I'm right, you'll need to keep a low profile until I'm ready."

CHAPTER EIGHT

AFTER A LONG night, feeling well-knackered, we went back to our respective rooms for some rest.

I was abruptly awakened by my cellphone. I knew it had to be Lexi since only Kovacs and she had my new number. Knuckling my eyes with one hand, I mumbled, "Hey Lexi, what time is it?"

"Nearly five PM," she replied.

"Five! It feels like I only just put my head down, and the phone rang. What's up?"

"I need to see you, Axis."

"When?"

"Tonight."

"Lexi, I need to speak with someone at Outlaw Productions. Can you give me a contact?"

"With who?"

"Someone at Outlaw." The phone fell silent. "You there, Lexi?" I could tell she had her hand over the phone, talking to someone else, and that raised suspicion.

"Sorry, Axis. My friend just asked me to invite you over for dinner."

I was relieved. "Okay, who is your friend?"

"An actress, Malika del Mundo... have you heard of her?"

"No, can't say I have, but that doesn't mean much. So, what about a contact at Outlaw?"

"Sorry, I left my cellphone at the house... oh wait a minute, Malika said she has the number. I'll call them and have someone call you."

"Okay, give them this number. And look, don't mention Kovacs or that Kincade is dead... got that? Just tell them I'm a film financier from Australia who has been dealing with your husband, and I need to talk to them about money. That should pique their interest."

"Okay. How about eight o'clock here for dinner?"

"Fine, just on my ace?"

"Ace?"

"Sorry, alone."

"Yes. I'll text you the address."

I jumped in the shower, wondering whether Lexi was on the level or not. But there was only one way to find out—I needed to spend some quality time quizzing her to see if she slips up. First, I needed to hear from the horse's mouth what happened to the opal, and that meant picking the brain of someone at Outlaw.

As I put the finishing touches on my attire, 'The Terrible Tango' broke the silence. A female Bronx accent greeted me on the other end.

"Hello, Mr Stone. I'm Rita Castellari, the production manager at Outlaw Productions. Miss Diamond called and said you wanted to speak to us about Mr Kincade's finances."

I put on my best banker's voice. "Yes, at your convenience, Miss Castellari."

"I can't help you myself, but I understand that you're in Hollywood. So, I've spoken with our agent there, Mr Rivers, and he can meet you. Where are you staying?"

"The Andaz Hotel on Sunset," I replied. "Um, I have a window at six today if he can make it."

"Maybe that'll work. Why don't you meet him in the lobby at that time?"

"Done. Um, how will I recognise him?" I asked.

"Oh, just identify yourself to the concierge, and Mr Rivers will ask for you to be pointed out."

"Sounds like you've done this before, Miss Castellari?"

"More often than I care to mention, Mr Stone. Thank you."

I immediately called Kovacs, told him about the meeting, and instructed him to stay put in his room. He was familiar with the actress Malika del Mundo.

"She is stunning," he said. "Her name means 'Queen of the World' in Spanish."

"I didn't know you could speak Spanish."

"Only ven it comes to a beautiful creature like her... Are you sure I can't accompany you to dinner?"

"No, sorry, mate. Have you heard of this guy Rivers?"

"No, Kincade never mentioned anyone at Outlaw. In fact, ze first time I heard of Outlaw was from you."

"Okay, I'll either talk to you later tonight, or I'll meet you in the lobby at eight-thirty in the morning, depending on whether I get lucky or not."

"With Malika, Lexi, or Rivers?"

"Sounds like a circus juggling act. Any one of them will do, but a threesome would be my preference."

To complete the illusion for the meeting with Rivers, I grabbed the instant card maker from my suitcase and printed off a couple of business cards. It's my favourite gadget, made in China, but then again, isn't everything? The size of a paperback novel and digital, it allows me to legitimately be whoever I want, whenever I want.

~ ~ ~

I spotted a guy in the lobby who had "Hollywood producer" or "gangster" written all over him, at least from my limited experience. It's tough to tell the difference. Dressed in a shiny grey suit over a white T-shirt, he had to be Rivers. As I approached him, I estimated his height at five-ten, with receding black hair. He appeared to be in his late thirties, probably of Italian or Spanish descent, which is quite common in this town. His eyes were fixed on the concierge, waiting for a tip about my identity. I guess I wasn't standing out as obviously as he was.

I walked up to him. "Mr Rivers... Axis Stone, Film Finances Australia."

We shook hands, and I noticed his handshake was limp-wristed. Maybe the chunky gold bracelet around his wrist was weighing his hand down. We exchanged business cards. I glanced at the Outlaw logo on his card—a cowboy's head with crossed smoking pistols—fitting, I thought. Rivers had a serious and somewhat grim look on his oversized face. There was nothing friendly about him at all. A noticeable scar dissected his left eyebrow, likely from a knife slash some years ago—a sign of an ill-spent youth, perhaps? More bling was draped around his neck. Upon closer inspection, he appeared more like a gangster than a Hollywood producer.

"Alcohol or coffee, Mr Rivers?" I asked.

"I'll take a coffee," he replied, his deep baritone voice laced with a sneer.

I led him to the Riot House Café, where we easily found a table since there were only a few customers. We sat down, and a waiter promptly approached us to take our order.

Leaning back in his chair and crossing his legs, Rivers stared at me before speaking gruffly, "So, Miss Castellari told me you've been working with Kincade?"

"Yes, he asked us for a bridging loan against his interest in a film that I believe your company is producing," I replied.

"And what film would that be?" he said, sounding smug.

"You're the production company, Mr Rivers. It's for you to say. I'm only interested in the deal—the equity, the security, the risk factor, and the ROI... return on investment."

"Yeah, I'm familiar with the term, Stone. So, why are you meeting me without Kincade? What would you want to know from me that he can't tell you himself?"

"Plenty. Carson Kincade is dead," I stated.

"Dead?" he questioned coolly. "So, what happened?"

"I understand from the police that he stopped a couple of bullets with the back of his head."

"Hmm, murder," he said far too easily for my liking, as though it were commonplace in Hollywood—maybe it is.

"I would have thought you'd be concerned, considering he was your partner," I pressed.

"And where did you get that idea, Stone?"

"Look, Mr Rivers, I'll level with you. Kincade told me he gave you an opal as security against a quarter of a million US dollars. We had already loaned him two hundred thousand that he had invested with you for script development. Now that he's dead, we'll be taking over his position. He told us that you only valued the opal at one hundred thousand, but we value it at two hundred and fifty thousand. So, we have an impasse."

"It doesn't mean much now that he's dead, does it?" he snarled churlishly.

"Actually, it means a hell of a lot—to us. So, either you give me the stone, or we accept the full value as further investment. If it's the latter, then paperwork will need to be drafted reflecting our equity in the film and the estimated returns, because we have a lien over the opal."

"Look, I didn't do any deal with Kincade. But I'll tell you this, if you can find a buyer for the opal at that price, then I don't see why we can't come to some sort of arrangement. Other than that, Kincade's attorney would be your best bet to discuss his estate."

The coffees arrived, interrupting our conversation.

"So, who do I need to speak to at Outlaw to close this?" I pushed.

"I'll get back to you on that," he said slowly.

His arrogance was irritating me.

"I'm only here for a couple of days, so how about using your phone to find out now?" I snapped.

He dumped three satchels of Equal sweetener into his coffee. "I do things at my own pace, Stone."

It was my turn to recline in the chair, cross my legs, and stink-eye him. "My meter is running," I growled. "I suggest you pick up your pace."

He returned my stare with interest, sipping on his cup of sweetener and coffee.

"What do you want, Stone?" he growled, obviously annoyed.

"Simple. The money or the opal."

"I'll pass on your request and get back to you," he said abruptly, then got to his feet.

My cellphone played 'The Terrible Tango', and I peered at it while speaking without looking up at Rivers. "Like I said, I haven't got long, and I really don't want to tell Detective Santana about the opal and Outlaw, or things might just get ugly."

That put the brakes on him.

It was a text from Lexi. Ignoring Rivers, I read the message to aggravate him even more.

He croaked icily, "Are you threatening me, Stone?"

I eyeballed him, refusing to show fear. The hostility between us was palpable. I decided to join in the game of angry surnames. "Call it what you like, Rivers. Just make sure you pass it on. I'm meeting Santana tomorrow morning for breakfast, and it would be in your best interests to get back to me before then."

I watched him storm out of the restaurant, leaving me with the tab. What a rude pig, with no bloody manners. He had just earned himself a bold, uppercase mention in my book of interest-bearing grudges.

~ ~ ~

After a quick change into smart casual attire, I was all set to take on Lexi Diamond and the Queen of the World for dinner.

Following the directions Lexi had texted me, I drove slowly along North Hillcrest Road in the Hollywood Hills, searching for a street number on a single-story white stucco bungalow. Unfortunately, almost every house on Hillcrest was a white stucco bungalow, hidden behind high security walls and overgrown vegetation that made house numbers almost impossible to read in the dark. I could imagine how Hiram Bingham must have felt exploring the wilds of the Andes Mountains looking for Machu Picchu. Eventually, I found the right number and drove up the steep, winding driveway to the house—better late than never.

A sensor light illuminated the big oak double doors for me to knock on. The door opened, revealing a maid in uniform. She confirmed that I was expected and led me into the hacienda-style house, along a terra cotta tiled hallway and through arches into a large, elegantly decorated living area. The furnishings were rich and luxurious, the best money could buy. We entered a dimly lit dining room that opened out through big sliding glass doors onto a patio and a glowing blue swimming pool. Standing by the pool, I spotted two of the most beautiful women I had ever seen, looking like a pair of Greek Goddesses.

"Ladies, I apologise deeply for my late arrival," I happily announced as I approached them. They turned from their conversation to face me.

Lexi held out her hand for me to shake. "Axis, we were worried about you."

I took her hand. "You two look like Athena and Aphrodite standing here under the serious moonlight."

"You see... I warned you, Malika. These Aussie men are hopeless romantics, just like Errol Flynn," Lexi said.

"And just as well proportioned," I jested.

Malika offered her hand, which I took and kissed.

"Pleased to meet you, Axis. Your reputation precedes you."

"I hope it's my best reputation and not the ugly one," I replied, locking eyes with the blue-eyed angel who possessed a figure of doom.

A nod from Malika, and I turned to find the maid standing behind me.

"What would you like to drink?" Malika asked, her accent offering no clues to its origin.

"Rye on the rocks, thanks."

Though I was in the land of the Harvey Wallbanger, one of my favourite drinks, I wasn't brave enough to order one just yet. The fear of excess vegetation had dampened my desire.

"I feel underdressed standing next to you angelic creatures. Malika, your accent, I can't quite—" I trailed off, captivated by her presence.

"I am originally from Rio de Janeiro," she almost moaned, rolling her tongue over the R's. At five foot ten, with long blue-black hair, cobalt-blue eyes, tanned skin, and the figure of Mamie Van Doren, she was the epitome of beauty. The girl standing next to her was drop-dead gorgeous, with a striking resemblance to Marilyn Monroe, but she lacked the pheromone sensuality and class that oozed from Malika. Malika truly lived up to her name, Queen of the World. My mind was summersaulting with possibilities, imagining what might be on the menu for the evening—I was hoping it would be me.

CHAPTER NINE

A FTER A WHILE, gliding as though floating inches above the ground, Malika led us inside to a lounge setting where we were served hors d'oeuvres. As we settled in, an odd feeling washed over me.

"Are you expecting somebody else?" I asked, trying to probe gently.

"Actually, we are, Axis. How perceptive of you... And if my hearing serves me well, he has just arrived," Malika replied with a hint of mystery. Before I could inquire further, Dorris, the maid, escorted him in.

He was around five foot ten, dressed in a dapper navy-blue suit that exuded class. With a neat cap of greying hair and a deep Mediterranean tan, he had the look of a refined gentleman. His bleak grey eyes, tight-lipped mouth, and the downward curve at the corners gave him an air of mystery. At first glance, he resembled Rivers, the man from Outlaw Productions I had met earlier at the Riot House. But this man exuded even more sophistication than Rivers could ever hope to possess. Both ladies stood up as he entered, indicating that he held a special place in their lives, for better or worse. He had that mysterious charm that I had always struggled to understand—charisma, they call it.

"Hi everyone, sorry I'm late, but hey, you know how it is in this town, everyone wants a piece of you," he said light-heartedly, if somewhat arrogantly. After exchanging European-style kisses with the ladies, he turned his attention to me. "So, who the hell is this?" he demanded with a gravelly voice.

"I'm Axis Stone," I replied cordially, offering my hand for a shake. I couldn't help but notice the four chunky gold rings adorning his fingers and the Paul Newman Rolex Daytona on his wrist. From my recollection, only two hundred of those watches had been produced. He was either loaded or flaunting a fake.

"I'm Al Head."

The realisation hit me like a ton of bricks. I felt like I had just shaken hands with the devil himself.

"Ah, I met your local agent, Mr Rivers, this afternoon," I said, still taken aback by the surprise. My mind raced, questioning why I had been kept in the dark about his arrival—was it intentional or simply an oversight? He gave me a look that promised a slow and painful demise.

"Sonny, yeah, yeah, I know," he replied dismissively.

We took our seats, and Dorris stood by to take his drink order.

"Give me rye on the rocks," he commanded, with a caustic tone.

At least he had good taste in drinks, I thought.

"I've just come from meeting him," he snarled.

It was evident that he held a high opinion of himself and a low opinion of every other male on the planet.

"An unnecessary meeting now that you're here, with Rivers having to defer decision-making to you," I stated firmly.

"Yeah, but my corporate protocol calls for Sonny to handle local matters. He didn't know you'd be making an offer that would require my authorisation," he explained.

I detected a New York accent, with just a hint of Italian, in his speech. Though his demeanour seemed friendly, it was clear that it was merely a facade. His eyes gave him away—sharp, flighty, piercing, and sinister. The guy was a gangster, just like his partner in crime, Sonny, and my bet was that they were part of the Mafia. The name Outlaw Productions suited them perfectly—it summed them up quite well.

"Please, no biz-talk, gentlemen. It is time to indulge ourselves," Malika interjected. "Dorris, tell di kitchen we are ready."

The maid promptly left for the kitchen. Throughout the evening, we discussed movies over three courses, with only a few subtle references to my line of work from Al, seemingly trying to corroborate my claim of being an Aussie film financier. The real test came during dessert, a crème soufflé.

"I've never heard of your company, Stone. Do you only finance Australian films?" Al inquired.

"No, we're known here as Media Funds Services," I lied, "and we've had a stake in several Hollywood productions. But yes, as you say, the majority of our investment portfolio consists of Australian films," I fabricated.

"I know a couple of Aussies in the game. Do you know Brenton Howard?" he asked.

I wagered that Brenton Howard was a fictional character he had conjured up to test my response.

"No, I've never heard of him," I replied.

I anticipated the next name would be real.

"How about Catherine Martin?" he inquired.

Fortunately, I kept myself well-informed about Australian celebrities, and she was one of them.

"I'm an aficionado of her production design. She did a fantastic job on 'Elvis'," I replied.

"Well, being married to Hugh Jackman would give her an edge," he remarked smugly.

"Not as much as being married to Baz Luhrmann," I corrected.

"Yeah, yeah, of course you're right," he agreed.

"Debra-Lee Furness is married to Hugh Jackman," Lexi chimed in.

"Too true," I said with a wry smile. "So, what's the title of the film that involved the late Carson Kincade, a person whom none of you seem to be mourning?"

I caught a sly glance exchanged between Al and Lexi, a glance that reeked of collusion.

"Yeah, well, he'll be missed, alright... old Carson. Let's raise our glasses to Carson Kincade," Al said as an afterthought.

We toasted in unison, "Carson Kincade."

"And the name of the movie?" I persisted.

Al hesitated for a moment. "Wait Until Dark," he finally revealed indignantly, as if reluctant to disclose the information. "But keep that to yourself for now."

"A remake of the Audrey Hepburn classic, no less. Quite a challenge to follow in her footsteps," I remarked.

"When you have two sparkling stars like the ones we have at our table tonight, it's not too difficult to expect that it'll be a huge success," he boasted with a fake grin.

"That's odd... Kincade told me Margot Robbie and Jamie Dornan were the main assets. Aren't they the reason for the rewrite?" I pressed.

"I think he might have been exaggerating. Why would we need to rewrite a remake?" he said dismissively.

"Then why would you need additional funds?" I countered.

"Because Jamie Dornan is all but attached. He just wants the screenplay updated some. It was, after all, made in nineteen sixty-seven, and the Alan Arkin character as the film's antagonist isn't so scary by today's standards."

"From memory, it was a Warner Brothers film. You must have pulled some strings to get the rights?" I delved.

He thought about it a moment. I could see the wheels turning in his mind.

"We bought the stage play adaptation rights. The writer Frederick Knott died in two thousand and two, and the rights passed to his family. He was an English playwright, probably better known for his London stage thriller Dial M for Murder that Hitchcock turned into a box office smash."

"Jamie Dornan will be perfect in ze supporting lead. He has that brooding cool about him," Malika said with a quiver of excitement in her voice.

"And he's oh-so-sexy," Lexi added with interest.

"Are you in the film as well, Malika?" I questioned.

"Maybe," she purred cutely.

"Tell me, Stone, what's the producer's offset from the Australian Government for film investment these days?" he queried.

It was a loaded question. I would be expected, as a film financier, to know the answer, but Axis Stone PI had no idea. There was a pregnant pause during which I carefully avoided eye contact with him and decided to sidestep answering the question. Instead, I offered up the only thing I thought could create a diversion.

"So, who murdered Carson Kincade, and why?"

By the expression on their faces, I'd thrown a timely spanner in the works. I was on a roll, if not a dangerous one.

"Which begs two further questions," I urged. "Is Lexi in danger, and is the murder connected to the film deal?"

"Now why would you say that, Stone?" Al grated in a derisive tone.

I waited a couple of beats for maximum impact.

"Because I'm having breakfast in the morning with Detective Santana in charge of the murder investigation, and he'll ask me what I know, that's why."

By his grimace, that had taken the wind out of his sails.

"I told you, Axis, Carson had a lot of enemies," Lexi maintained, a little uptight.

"Do we really have to talk about this at ze dinner table, gentlemen?" Malika requested.

Al rocked back in his chair and folded his arms across his chest defensively.

"You know, buddy, I have my doubts about you being who you say you are. You mouth off more like a cop."

I opened my coat. "Look, I'm not wearing a wire, Al. I'm sure you're normally an excellent judge of character, but no... this time you've got the bull by the tail."

His grey eyes looked even bleaker for a moment, then he snarled almost under his breath, "You've got a big mouth, Stone."

"What is this 'bull by ze tail'?" Malika asked Lexi, who shrugged her shoulders.

"Look at it another way, who stands to gain the most out of Kincade's death?" I pressed.

"There's no need to continue this conversation," Al complained. "You can tell Detective Santana whatever you want. You've already tried to threaten Sonny and now me. Drop it, Stone. It would be better for your health, capiche?"

The naked savagery in his voice sent a chill up my spine, so I backed off a little but still needed to probe deeper.

"Tell me, Al, how did you come up with a valuation of only a hundred large for an opal worth more than twice that?" I needled.

He unfolded his arms, broke the barrier, leaned forward, collected his glass of wine from the table, and then took a sip. Relaxing back in his chair, he eyeballed me and then said with a sigh, "We had it appraised by a prominent jeweller in Vegas."

I continued in an even more casual tone. "Because the way I see it, we can do one of two things: you can either keep the opal at its real value, with my people taking Kincade's total equity position in the film, or you can give it back, and we walk away."

"That would leave me out of pocket a hundred large. Why would I wanna do that?" he snarled.

I decided to call his bluff. "Then it has to be the equity position."

"If you think the opal is worth two fifty, then sell the damn thing and give me a hundred grand, and you're out."

"That would leave me out of pocket a hundred thousand. No thanks," I snapped back.

"What if I tell you to go to hell... what will you do then, Stone?" he growled, shaking his head contemptuously.

It was my turn to rock back in my chair. I said stiffly, "Simple, I'd let Detective Santana settle the score for me."

It was a Mexican standoff, or more so, a dinner party glare-off. We sat with our eyes locked, contesting to see who would be the first to blink. Malika broke the stalemate.

"Now, now, gentlemen," Malika said, trying to defuse the tension. "Let's not spoil ze evening. I'm sure zere is a way to settle this."

"There is, sweetheart, but it might leave a mess on your nice clean floor," Al growled.

"Don't worry, Al, she's got a maid to clean up your mess," I countered.

"You don't seem to be taking me very seriously, Stone!" The last word came out in a full-throated roar.

"Don't bark at me like a rabid Sicilian dog, pal," I growled. "Stand-over merchants don't impress me one little bit. Either we cut a deal now or I walk, leaving you to deal with the consequences."

"You've got balls, Stone, I'll give you that much, but I warn you... don't push me."

"Okay," I stood up, threw my napkin on the table. "I'm no one's piñata, Head. Thank you for a lovely dinner, Malika."

"Sit down!" Al barked.

I froze and glared at him. "I guess you missed the bit about stand-over merchants and a piñata," I said slowly.

I knew I was pushing the envelope with this bloke, and he was about to blow his stack. But I felt he expected me or anyone else, for that matter, to simply cave in to his intimidation. By my reckoning, if I did that, I'd be unlikely to make it back to my hotel in one piece.

Head glared at the host. "Malika, take Lexi out by the pool, tell Dorris to bring me a bottle of rye. I need to talk to this guy in private."

Malika begrudgingly obliged. I sat back down, glad my ruse had worked. Once we were alone, his tone changed to an even more sinister one.

He slapped me playfully on the shoulder and said with a false laugh, "It's not often I let anyone stand up to me. You're all right,

Stone... like I said, you've got balls. I could use a guy like you. Whatever they pay you, I'll double it?"

I knew he meant it, but I chose to pass. It would be like working for Hitler.

"Let's talk about that some other time, Al. For now, we need to cut a deal."

"You see? That's what I admire — loyalty."

Dorris arrived with a bottle of JD, two glasses, and a bucket of ice.

Al reached into his inside coat pocket. I thought for a moment he was going for a piece, but he pulled out a couple of cigars instead.

"Cuban, want one?" he said with a smirk.

"H. Upmann number two Reserva and a JD on ice, how could a bloke refuse?" I said.

"Hmm, you know your stuff." He rolled the cigar between his fingers up to his ear to listen for its freshness, then bit off the end and spat it irreverently onto the floor.

I followed suit without spitting mine. He pulled a gold Dunhill cigarette lighter from his pocket, flicked it open, and allowed me to roll the cigar in the naked flame, sucking on it until it was well alight. He lit his own, took a big drag, and exhaled a column of smoke through his nose and mouth.

"Excellent. Now look down here," he said around the cigar clenched in his bite.

He had a nine mil Glock on his lap aimed at my stomach.

He snarled, "This will make a noise, and the mess on the floor I was talking about... the mess won't matter to you because you'll be sucking in your last gulps of air while your punctured lung fills with blood. Oh, by the way, the exit wound in your back will be the size of a dinner plate. Get the picture?"

"That's not your form, Al... you only shoot people in the back of the head... two bullets, right? Now, if I were you, I'd take a look here." I nodded at my lap and the knife I'd taken from the table while he was busy fishing for the Dunhill lighter in his pocket.

"You win with the Glock and the exit wound, but I take you with me because I'll gut you with one quick swipe. So, what'll it be, Al?" I challenged.

CHAPTER TEN

AL CHUCKLED AROUND his cigar while slipping the Roscoe back in his kick. Then he rocked back in his chair and took a long drag of his cigar.

"Something amuses you?" I said dully.

"Any normal guy would have shit his boxers having a gun pointed at him but not you." He leaned forward, eyeballed me and dropped his voice a tone. "The only way you learn to handle that is from the sort of experience you don't get financing goddamned films."

"First of all, I don't wear boxers. Second, I'm the guy they call in to collect outstanding debts and to investigate shonky deals," I countered.

"Shonky? ... That must be an Aussie word," he snapped.

"Scams, fraud, shams, snow jobs – whatever you like to call it ... still adds up to be a shonk."

"You Aussies are a weird mob," he chuckled.

"That'd make a good title for a movie and yeah, we Aussies have a word for everything, especially a hit, did you order Kincade whacked?" I asked, trying to catch him off guard.

"No, but I'm not unhappy someone did," he snorted.

"You stand to gain most from his death," I argued.

He countered quickly, "No, that'd be Lexi."

"Okay, that brings us back to the opal." I said, putting the knife back on the table.

"You're starting to bother me Stone."

"Yeah, I get that a lot ... don't be a wet blanket Head, put up with it. So, here's the problem in a nutshell Al, Kincade bought the opal for two fifty large with a ten grand deposit and a credit note for the remainder. He gave the stone to you as an investment in your film. You devalued the investment to a hundred grand. Kincade defaulted on the credit note – the owner of the stone wants his money. Kincade offered film shares in payment but only to the tune of a hundred grand. The owner called us in to value the film shares. Kincade gets himself rubbed out, so we either get two fifty grand equity in a film guaranteed to be made or we get the opal back. What'll it be?"

"I've got no problem with giving you equity against an investment but the investment is a quarter of a mill and the stone ain't worth more than a hundred gees," he argued, shrugging his shoulders and parting his hands repentantly.

The time had arrived to implement my plan. "What if I get a second appraisal from a name jeweller to confirm its value at a quarter of a mill?"

He took a deep drag of his cigar, thought for a few beats then spoke breathing smoke like a dragon. "The stone still has to be turned into cash, and unless your name jeweller wants to buy it—"

I cut him off, "That might be on the cards."

"Okay, look-it ... if that's the case then we might have a deal. I'll set it up for Sonny to get you the opal and give you seven days to sell it. You commit to invest a quarter of a mill with Outlaw once it's sold. In the meantime, you say nothing to the cops about the opal or the film. Agreed?"

Eyeballing him I rasped, "Sounds doable, but I'll need paperwork."

"And I'll need security for the stone," he added sharply.

I had it for him. "Sonny can personally bring the stone to the Beverly Hills jeweller, so it doesn't go out of his sight."

G. L. Keady

He was nodding slowly. I figured I'd achieved something. I might have missed out on the ménage à trois but I'd got the cigar. I wasn't sold that Al would go through with the deal, I'd just have to wait and see. In the meantime, I needed to come up with a way of covering my butt at the meeting with Detective Santana. There was no doubting Head was a crook, he wouldn't have pulled a piece on me if he wasn't, but whether he had Kincade knocked off — well, the jury was out on that one — but he was the most likely candidate and more than likely arranged the hit.

Lexi walked me to the Mustang. I grabbed her by the shoulders and fixed my eyes on hers. "Listen babe, you better meet me at Denny's at nine in the morning," I pressed.

"Why?"

"Because if you don't Detective Santana will have half the LAPD out chasing your pretty butt."

"I don't know if Al will let me—"

"What?" I snapped. "Does this guy control you or something?"

"What can I tell Santana he doesn't already know?"

I watched her nervously chewing on the knuckle of her right index finger.

"Just tell him what you told me. You had a fight, went upstairs, heard a gunshot, ran out of the house and saw a guy escape into a waiting car. That's about the box and dice, isn't it?" I said.

"Two gunshots, but yeah," she sniffled. "I was afraid the killer had seen me. So, I jogged to the Canyon Country Store on Laurel Canyon and phoned Malika. She came and picked me up."

"What time was that?"

"Just after midnight."

"You sure?"

"Of course."

I wasn't convinced, her eyes were a dead giveaway. She quickly threw her arms around me and began to weep. "Axis, I don't know what I would do without you. I'm scared of Al. Do you think he's on the level?" she asked.

It was an Oscar-winning performance and I knew it. "Put it this way kid … I'd stay well clear of him if I were you," I warned.

"But I need somebody," she said, flashing her cobalt blue eyes at me coyly.

"Yeah, it's nice to be needed, not even the tide would take me out when I was a teenager," I joked.

"You're crazy," she giggled cutely.

I gave her a hug. She smelt good. I held her at arm's length and eyeballed her. "Remember what you said about cigar smoking producers taking advantage of you? Hmm?" I left her with the thought punctuated by a sceptical smile.

~ ~ ~

I was feeling pretty good driving down Laurel Canyon with the wind in my hair — on top of the world, you might say. As I passed the Canyon Country Store, I noticed it was closing. A check of the dash clock confirmed it had just gone eleven. I recalled Lexi saying she'd called Malika from the Country Store at midnight. Odd, I thought — it would have been closed.

When I got to my hotel room, I phoned Kovacs. It took a while for him to answer, and when he did, his voice was croaky.

"Hey Kozzi, did I wake you?"

"Yes, vat time is it for Christ's sake?" he grumbled.

"Just past eleven … listen, we need to talk before we meet Santana in the morning."

He came to my room, and I filled him in on the events of the evening. The key issue was to get him to agree to the plan I'd concocted. It took a couple of JDs, but I eventually got him on board. I was a little concerned when he told me he'd got a call from Mansfield looking to confirm the rumour Kincade had been murdered. That meant the word was out. During their brief conversation, Mansfield had mentioned both the opal and Outlaw productions for the first time. We agreed there was a chance he might know more than we had initially figured.

~ ~ ~

When we arrived at Denny's the next morning, Detective Santana was already on his second coffee. We sat at the table he'd been holding and ordered breakfast. Santana reckoned the eggs Benedict was to die for, and being the head of homicide, I expected he'd know, so I ordered it. He wasn't wrong. We eventually got around to discussing the case.

"The letter opener turned up. You were right, it had blood work and we lifted prints," he said in his Latino drawl.

"Whose blood?" I asked.

"Not Kincade's."

"Whose prints?"

"Kincade's," he confirmed.

Kovaks asked, "From zat, can we assume you haf ze blood type of ze murderer?"

"Yes, but it leads us nowhere unless we can match it with a suspect," he attested.

I was expecting Lexi and checked the time … it was a quarter of ten … she was late.

Santana asked, "There's word Kincade was involved with some dubious types on a film deal, do you know anything about that?"

"Nothing more than you would," I said, trying to dodge the question.

"You didn't get to know Kincade through an Internet dating service, so what was it?" he posed, losing patience.

I sat back defensively. "I told you — I'm on a case."

"Yeah, I got that but it's time you came clean with the goddamned truth because if you don't … well, let just say things might get ugly for you. You're trying my patience, son."

"Okay, okay, Kincade needed capital to invest in a film. Kovacs here brokered a deal, and my client provided a gemstone to be used as collateral. Kincade paid a deposit for the stone and gave a credit note for the remainder — it's still bouncing. My client wants payment in full or the gemstone returned, that's my gig."

"Right. Now at least we're on the same page. I guess you're talking about the opal?"

I was surprised. "How long have you known about it?"

"Long enough, now listen-up, you and Kovacs have gotta get out of town and let the law handle this. If you stay, you'll end up on a mortuary slab. There's a lot more to this case than you know. What you've been messing with is only the tip of the iceberg. This is a sting worth in the vicinity of fifty million dollars or more. Kincade is only one of the victims. We had another murder a couple of weeks back that we think is related."

"Are you saying someone is selling shares in a film that will never be made and killing anyone who gets in the way?" I submitted.

"You've got it in one," he confirmed.

"Are zey targeting other has-been producers like Kincade?" Kovacs urged.

"Sure, and others out for a quick buck," Santana confirmed. "I think you better inform your client that the chances of him getting his money or that stone back are next to squat."

"He's not going to like that," I grumbled.

Just then I got a tap on the shoulder, turned around sharply, and found Lexi standing there in all her majesty. After introducing her to Santana, she sat down and I told her to repeat what she'd told me about the night of the murder. Santana took it all on board and then advised her she needed to accompany him downtown to make a formal statement and answer a few more questions.

After Santana had left with Lexi, we sat there stunned, our plan was in tatters after his ultimatum.

"I thought getting run out of town was reserved for Hollywood westerns," I groaned.

"Zis is a bloody Hollywood western. But does he haf ze authority to enforce it?" Kovacs argued.

"I don't know Kozza, maybe ... but I think he'd need US immigration on his side."

"Unless he pulls ze terrorist card," he grated.

"To be honest, I think he was just telling us that for our own good. But we can't ignore his warning, he'd know if this thing is bigger than we thought, and by the way ... how in the hell did he know about the opal?"

"We're down to making a choice, either we stay and see your plan through or we bail out," Kovacs summed up. "But zere'll be hell to pay from Gary and Rod if we go back empty-handed."

"Okay, let's head back to the hotel, I need to sit by the pool and get my head together."

~ ~ ~

There was a bit more scenery poolside this time, but my mind was way too occupied to appreciate it. I hit the pool and swam half a dozen laps, hoping the exercise might trigger a Eureka moment, but it didn't. While drying myself down, my cellphone rang. It was Lexi with a message from Al Head. My friend with all the bad manners, Sonny Rivers, would meet me in the hotel lobby at midday ... He'd have the item with him. The cloak and dagger stuff totally unnecessary because Lexi made it clear she knew what was going on.

"What are you and Kovacs up to, Axis? Why is Sonny bringing you the opal?" she quizzed.

"We're getting another valuation, don't worry about it, honey," I said convincingly.

"Axis, I've just been grilled for an hour by your detective friend and his zombie sidekick Slim Pickins—"

"Williams," I corrected.

"Yeah, him ... and you're telling me not to worry? They let me go with the old 'don't leave town because you're a suspect' rave. I went there thinking I was a possible victim, and I left being the friggin' suspect!"

The last two words came in such a squeal I had to hold the phone away from my ear to avoid permanent ear damage.

"Want me to pick you up?" I said, trying to calm her down.

"No!" she snapped. "Malika is here, and we're on our way to her place. Santana said you're leaving for Sydney, but you're meeting Sonny ... I don't get it, Axis, what's going on?"

"I'll explain later. Is Al still in town?"

"No, he went back to Vegas."

Her answer sounded like a lie.

"Which of you is bonking him?"

"Does it matter?" she snarled dismissively.

"No, I guess it doesn't because you just answered that."

"Is there ever a time when you're not thinking about sex, Axis?"

"Yeah, back when I thought the only thing that came out of my penis was pee."

She sniggered, "You're a basket-case, Axis."

She got the last word in and then terminated the call. The expression on Kovacs' face said it all.

"Ze only thing zat came out of my penis was pee? Vat ze hell was zat about?"

"Don't ask, mate ... Rivers will be in the lobby at midday. I guess that's made the decision for us. We'll go ahead with the plan."

"You sure?"

"It's the only option we've got left, isn't it?"

Kovacs threw open his hands penitently, "Yeah, I suppose you're right."

I pressed urgently, "We've got an hour and a half to get our act together, we better get a move on."

CHAPTER ELEVEN

I WAS SITTING in the hotel lobby reading the LA Times when I sighted Rivers. He was an hour late, and when he got to me, he didn't have the courtesy to apologise.

"You have the merchandise?" I said sourly.

"Yeah, so what's next?" he grumbled.

"Well, apart from sitting on my butt waiting for you for the last hour, there's a gem expert who's been waiting patiently at the Mondrian Hotel for me to call."

"So, call him," he said smugly.

I dialled Kovacs, eyeballing Rivers with loathing.

I talked loud for his benefit. "Hello, Mr Stein, I apologise for being late. Yes, I understand you're a busy man. Do you still have time to meet us? At the Skybar? Excellent, we'll be there in five minutes. Thank you, Mr Stein. Goodbye."

We left Andaz, crossed over Sunset, and after a short walk, entered the lobby of the Mondrian Hotel. We took the elevator to the Rooftop Bar. It was empty except for Kovacs, who was occupying one corner.

He was dressed for the occasion in a suit and a pair of off-the-shelf reading glasses. We joined him.

"Hello, Mr Stein, I'd like you to meet Mr Rivers," I said cordially.

"Pleased to meet you, Mr Rivers," Kovacs announced with an excellent Hungarian accent. "I am Saul Stein." He handed Rivers a business card that I'd produced for him earlier. "Please sit down, can I order you a drink?"

"No ... your card says gemmologist ... you're supposed to be a buyer!" Rivers rasped with a hangover in his voice.

"That was not what I agreed to with Al. We are to get a second appraisal from a quality jeweller, and that's Mr Stein here," I said calmly.

"Mr Rivers, I can value ze stone, and if it is a viable prospect, I can provide buyers."

"Okay, okay, we do that," he said, irritably fumbling inside his coat pocket to ultimately come up with a black leather jewellery box. He handed it over to Kovacs, who produced a jeweller's loop from his side pocket, opened the box, and then peered at the contents through the magnifying lens. Even from where I was sitting, I could see the radiant play of colours from the oval-shaped stone.

"Ah, yes, yes, a Queensland black boulder opal of ze finest quality ... no flaws, no scratches, an amazing display of colour, harlequin in pattern ... extremely rare." He removed the loop from his eye and peered at Rivers. "I am honoured to see such a fine specimen, once in a lifetime you get ze opportunity to see a stone of such rare quality."

"Yeah, yeah, yeah, cut the blag, what's it worth?" Rivers grated irritably like he had somewhere else to go.

"I must weigh it first," Kovacs said, putting down the loop. He picked up his briefcase, opened it, took out a small set of digital scales, and weighed the opal.

"Hmm, it weighs twenty-four point seven carats. At I would say ten thousand dollars per carat, if it was to go to auction or for insurance purposes—"

"Two hundred and forty-seven thousand dollars?" I calculated.

"Zat is quite correct, Mr Stone," Kovacs said with a big grin.

"That's great, but what can you get for it? Like anything, it's only worth what you can sell it for," Rivers growled impolitely.

It was the most prophetic thing to come out of his gob so far.

"I could sell it for two hundred and twenty-five thousand dollars, less my ten percent commission, so in your hand, roughly two hundred and two thousand." He put his tools away, and then handed the stone in its box back to Rivers. "I will go to ze bathroom while you discuss it."

"Before you go, how long to sell it?" Rivers questioned.

"Um, no longer zan a week or so," Kovacs said offhandedly, and then marched off to the bathroom.

Rivers was thinking long and hard.

"No need to give him an answer right away. He's in town a couple of days, but if Al wants to double what he's been offered, then I suggest you get back to me by tomorrow."

He tucked the box away inside his suit coat, stood up, and growled, "You'll be hearing from me, Stone."

"My cell number is on my business card. I'll be leaving in a couple of days."

He nodded slowly and then walked out. I sat back relieved and loosened my necktie. I hate wearing those things; they strangle you.

A moment later Kovacs cruised back to the table, sporting a grin like he'd just won the lottery.

"Hey, mate, how was zat for an Oscar-winning performance? Tell me he bought ze act."

"Nar, mate, he stormed out the bloody door ... didn't believe a damn thing you said. Overacting, mate, no subtlety — you need to study the method, my friend."

"But, but!" Kovacs protested, his eyes the size of dinner plates.

I couldn't hold back any longer and crowed with a massive grin, "Nar, it was a command performance, mate, he came in spinner! Now, let's have that drink."

"Not here ... zis is costa del fortune. Besides, I had to bullshit my way in."

"Okay, so back to the Riot House for lunch by the pool, your shout."

Before he could raise an objection, I was halfway out the door.

~ ~ ~

Again, the rooftop pool was void of spectator sport. Disgruntled, I lowered myself into a deckchair under a big lime green Perrier beach umbrella and waited for Kovacs. He turned up a few minutes later.

"Hey, Kozzi, sit down, we need to tighten up our plan."

He threw open his hands in disapproval. "Hey, vat's dis Kozzi thing?"

"Don't make a fuss, mate. You know us Aussies, we love nicknames ... yours is Kozzi."

He sat down, thinking about it. "Vat's yours, den?"

"Handsome will do just fine... Hey mate!" I yelled to attract the busboy to order.

"Handsome?" Kozzi repeated, frowning.

After some grub and a few drinks, we had a new plan. It wasn't the best, but it was all we could come up with given the time. The pool attendant brought the hands-free with a call for me.

"Hello, ah, Detective Santana, how you going?... We're by the hotel pool soaking up some of your magnificent Californian rays. You're nearby? Okay sure, drop in." I handed the phone back to the attendant and glared at Kovacs. "I don't like him cold-calling us like that... he's up to something."

"Yeah, like trying to solve a murder or two."

"I get that, but I've got a gut feeling something else is up."

I took a quick dip to refresh myself.

The weather is pretty much the same every day in L.A., monotonous some might complain, but for me, it was nothing short of divine. By the time I'd dried myself down, Santana and Williams were there.

I greeted them, "Sit down, gentlemen, how about a cold beer?"

They remained standing, tight-lipped. "No, we just had our chow thanks," Santana said with a dour look on his face.

"We're here on business Stone," Williams said gruffly.

"Sounds grim by the formality of it," I observed.

Williams handed me a document... it looked legal. It was notification from the US Immigration Department that our visas were to be temporarily suspended.

"I requested your visas to be suspended today but had to settle for tomorrow," Williams said with a smirk, glad to be getting rid of us.

I handed the notice to Kovacs.

"We might need to speak to our consulate, is this our copy?" I asked politely.

"Yes, it won't reflect on your immigration record like a black mark or anything, I think that's spelt out clear enough, but due to the circumstances we took this action for your own good," Santana stated with a concise tone. The friendliness towards us had evaporated from Santana's demeanour.

"Considerate of you, is this normally how you treat law-abiding citizens from a foreign country visiting your shores — run them out of town like in a John Wayne Western?" I snarled resentfully.

"Zis is a travesty of justice," Kovacs added. Being a devout socialist, he was angry about any kind of persecution.

"Think of the upside, you'll get free tickets out of here to wherever you want," Williams said with a cheesy grin.

I fired back at him coldly, "We already have return tickets."

"Well then, you'll get to live another day, and you'll get a police escort to LAX right onto the plane just to make sure," he returned serve.

"Just what I always wanted," I muttered cynically.

"We'll be in touch," Williams concluded and then sauntered off.

Santana stayed, looking contrite. "Sorry fellas, but you will appreciate this once you eventually learn what you've been caught up in."

We watched them leave.

"Vill I call ze Aussie Consulate?" Kovacs offered.

"Nah, let's just roll with the punches."

Kovacs didn't seem impressed with the ultimatum, but as far as I was concerned, it was all going according to plan.

Later in my room, 'The Terrible Tango' shattered the silence. It was Sonny Rivers, he'd spoken to Al Head, and he'd agreed to give Stein the opal, but only if I handed over my passport as security. I agreed. We arranged to catch up in the hotel lobby at ten the next morning. I immediately phoned the Australian Consulate and reported my passport lost. Then I decided to cold-call Lexi at Malika's home.

~ ~ ~

I knocked on the door, and it opened. "Malika, I was expecting Dorris," I said surprised.

"Nice to see you, Axis," she said in a soft voice. I loved the sexy way she pronounced my name.

"It is the day off for Dorris."

"Mind if I come in?"

She opened the door wider for me to walk past her into the living room. Her dress was the colour of sandalwood, strapless, hugging her waist, then flaring recklessly down to her knees. Her perfume had all the subtle delicacy of an atomic bomb.

"To what do I owe your visit, Axis?" she asked lightly.

"Surely such a beautiful woman doesn't require a reason from me?"

"Oo, I am so flattered," she said coyly, fanning her face descriptively with an open hand.

She walked over to the couch and relaxed into it gracefully. The dress cooperated, giving a little here, tightening a little there. I sat in a wicker armchair opposite her.

"I actually came to speak to Lexi, she seemed upset when we spoke earlier today."

"Lexi is not here."

"Oh, has she returned home?"

"No, Axis, Lexi is in Vegas."

"Vegas? ... but?"

"I know, the police told her not to leave town, but she went with Al."

"Al Head? ... I thought he'd already left?"

"You did not know they are an item?"

It was a surprise. Sometimes, when it comes to the fairer sex, I miss the obvious by a country mile.

"She said she was going to call you or your friend at the hotel."

I got up and paced the floor, mulling over this new revelation and the consequences of it. Then I sat down beside her.

"How long have they been an item?"

"Oh, quite a while, that's why Al was here. After the murder, he came to take her back to Vegas with him once she'd given her statement to the police."

She was suddenly a lot closer than she had been a moment before. Her eyes were clear, limpid blue, and her lips puckered provocatively. So, being the hell-raiser that I am, I kissed her. There was no resistance... in the moment before our lips met, she had waved a white flag, unconditionally surrendering. After the kiss, her eyelids opened slowly and then fluttered a couple of times.

"Axis," she said huskily. "Do you know what you do to a girl?"

"I'm certain you know what you do to a man," I said smoothly.

She closed her eyes again. "More," she purred, "please?"

"Let's relax for a while," I suggested. "Tempting as your offer is, I need time to consider it."

"Axis!" she said coyly. "Do I frighten you?"

"Just curious," I told her. "I haven't kissed a real-live movie star before."

"There's no reason to be afraid of that. I'm an excellent performer."

"Yes, well, I certainly have you figured as a true artiste."

With a simple move, her dress fell open, and I felt the pliant warmth of her body pressing against me. I slipped off my coat, unbuttoned my shirt... her lips quivered against mine. She wanted me as bad as I wanted her — for a brief moment, I wondered about making Hollywood my home — then, I lost the capacity for thinking any longer. She suddenly took her arms from around my neck, pulled the front of her dress closed, and backed away, trembling uncontrollably.

"I need a drink," she stammered huskily.

She stayed on the couch while I made the drinks. The living room was quite dark with just one light over the bar — the bottles all nicely grouped, the ice bucket full and glistening. When I re-joined her, she was half-lying across one corner of the couch, displaying a long section of bare thigh.

She smiled lazily as she took the drink. "Thank you, darlink."

Coming from her sensuous lips, the word darlink was seriously exotic.

"Here's to us," I proposed.

She lifted her glass and toasted, "I'll drink to that!"

I watched her take a sip, her black hair making a soft frame for the unblemished oval of her face. Even in the semi-darkness of the room, her brown, delicately textured skin shone with a pearly luminescence like I'd never seen on anyone before.

She looked at me with bedroom eyes, suddenly conscious of my gaze, and then smiled brilliantly. "Come, darling, sit here," she purred, patting the couch gently with her fingers. I obeyed like a puppy.

She put down her drink and then gently kissed me. "Umm, I like," she whispered, and from that moment on, the battle was lost. I put down my drink.

CHAPTER TWELVE

I **KISSED HER** at the front door. Peering into her beautiful, smiling eyes, I asked, "Did Lexi say when she would be back?"

"Remind me again, darlink... who is Lexi?" She grinned, sheepishly.

"Exactly. You've got my number, give me a call when and if you feel the urge," I said softly.

"I'm feeling ze urge already."

Convinced I couldn't go another round, I climbed into the Mustang and sped off to the Andaz Hotel.

~ ~ ~

The next morning, just as I was about to leave the hotel room to meet Kovacs at Denny's for breakfast, the house phone rang. It was Rivers, wanting to meet for the exchange. I set the Andaz lobby at ten a.m. as the rendezvous point, and he agreed. I fetched my passport from the room safe and rang Kovacs.

I told him to stay in his room while I met up with Rivers. If Rivers happened to catch sight of him, the game would be up. Just as I hung up, the message light flicked on. It was from the Australian Consulate advising that my new passport was ready for collection. Satisfied, I went down to the lobby to meet Rivers.

This time, he impressed me by arriving on time. I swapped my passport for the jewellery box, checked that The Pride was inside, and then slipped it into the inner pocket of my dark blue Hugo Boss Arwido blazer.

He moved closer, eyeballed me, and all but whispered, "You've got a week, Stone. If it gets done sooner, call me. You've got my number. I don't trust you, Al might, but not me."

"That only goes to prove how much more class Al's got than you, Sonny," I retorted.

He moved even closer and growled angrily, "Very funny, asshole. If something goes wrong with this deal, I'll personally take it out on you!"

His breath was so bad I recoiled. "Okay, Rivers, I get your point, but do something about your breath, will you? It smells like you've gargled sewage."

Ignoring me, he turned on his heel and stormed off.

"Hey, Rivers!" I called after him.

He stopped. I caught up with him. "Take this," I said, handing him a business card.

He rolled his eyes. "You got Alzheimer's or something? I've got it already?"

"Yeah, but this one's got my new cell number. Call me if you need me because I'm checking out of here later today."

A look of dissatisfaction crossed his gnarly face. He strode towards me, got in my face, and grated, "Wait a minute, that wasn't part of the goddamned deal!"

"Hey, where I choose to stay has nothing to do with the goddamned deal... You've got my passport, I can't skip the country... Now get out of my face!"

He stepped closer and poked me in the chest with his finger. "Ring me with your new address, you hear me, Stone? Ring me... today!"

I pinched my nose and held my breath, "Mate, your breath is seriously off! I'd see a doctor about halitosis if I were you."

He turned on his heel and stormed out of the hotel.

I chuckled to myself and went back to my room. The message light was on again. I played it.

"Axis, this is Lexi." She sounded furious. "It was all getting too much for me to stay in L.A., especially with you sleeping with my friend... I'll try Kovacs' room in case he's there... I need to vent to someone. Goodbye, you low bastard!"

Her angry parting words hit me like a ton of bricks. She was with Al, and totally pissed about my fling with Malika. Now it was likely she'd expose our cover and tell Al about Kovacs. I quickly dialled Kozzi to warn him.

The same idea had occurred to him after Lexi had unloaded on him as promised.

"Your sex life seems to get you into plenty of trouble, Axis," Kovacs declared with a snigger.

"Kozzi, what can I do when a stunning, sexy woman like Malika throws herself at me?"

"Get on with ze job," he said smugly.

"Yeah, well, I did. Anyhow, I've got to go downtown to collect my replacement passport."

"Zat was quick. Who do you know at ze Aussie consulate?"

"No-one, I guess they're just efficient here..."

"Zat's a first. You have ze Pride?"

"Yes, so we go through with the plan. I'll bring it to you now."

I hung up the phone, ducked next door, and knocked. Kovacs opened it, dressed only in his underwear.

"Jesus, mate, I didn't know anyone wore boxer shorts like those anymore," I joked.

"Come in, I'm packing."

I handed him the jewellery box.

"Listen... stay put here until the cops arrive to escort you to LAX. Tell them I'm already at the airport waiting for you, alright?"

He nodded. "I had a conference call with Gary and Rod, told zem we got ze Pride. Zey're pleased with vat we accomplished. Rod said he might haf a buyer for ze stone in Tokyo and will honour our commission. Zey asked ven you'll be back in Sydney?"

"Good. I'll call them when the coast is clear. It's not over until that Qantas flight has you and The Pride at forty thousand feet en route to Sydney."

"I hear you," he confirmed.

I held out my hand to shake. "Okay, my friend, it's been cool working with you."

We shook hands and hugged.

He held me at arm's length, eyeballed me, then said with genuine concern, "Be careful, mate. I know it's better for us to split up and for you to follow later, but you've got no-one to votch your back once I'm gone."

"Don't worry about me, Kozzi, I get paid for doing this sort of shit. Safe flight. No doubt we'll have a beer or ten when we catch up in Sydney."

I went down to the lobby and checked out. Then I took my bag to the Mustang.

~ ~ ~

The drive to the Aussie Consulate in Century Park East gave me time to think, and let me tell you…I had plenty to think about. If Lexi had blown the whistle, which was more than likely, how would Al react? I needed to put myself in his shoes to figure that out. Just as I was entering the car park of the 2029 building, I realised the only weak link in the plan was the gap between me leaving the hotel and Kozzi waiting for the police to escort him to the airport. Would Al arrange for someone to whack Kovacs or me or both during that time? But then again, he'd need to have inside information to know the timing of it. My phone hadn't rung from Rivers, so that made me think the shit hadn't hit the fan yet. But then again, would Rivers phone me?

~ ~ ~

I went through the ground floor security checks, was given a mask, and then took the elevator to the Consulate level. There, I paid an exorbitant fee, collected the new passport, and was out of the joint inside half an hour. I thought to phone Kozzi to check on him, but my gut was telling me to get back to the Andaz Hotel A.S.A.P. Experience had taught me to listen to my gut, but I'd need to avoid the cops turning up there expecting to find me.

~ ~ ~

I decided to slip in the back door of the Andaz, through the kitchen and into the service elevator. Amazingly, I achieved that without attracting any attention. I got out on my floor and hoofed it to Kozzi's door. I knocked and it swung open. I immediately saw Kozzi lying face down on the floor in a pool of blood. There were two bullet holes in the back of his skull—he'd been shot in the same execution style as Kincade. I didn't turn him over…it would have been too gruesome.

Overcome with grief, I slumped onto the bed with my face in my hands. "Ah Kozzi," I groaned dispiritedly. "What the hell happened, mate?" It struck me I was loitering—I needed to get out of there before the cops arrived—and I needed to leave no trace of having been there. The room had been turned over. It took a large step to avoid the pool of blood that had grown larger on the floor, and that told me Kozzi had met his fate only twenty minutes or so before I got there. As I reached the door, I heard a distant ding—an elevator had arrived on the floor, probably full of cops to escort us to the airport. It dawned on me I was forgetting something important. "The Pride!" I growled to myself through gritted teeth.

Moving at light speed, I hopped back over the pool of blood and then scanned the room for Kossi's briefcase. I found it open on the bathroom floor with its contents spilled. I was hoping The Pride hadn't been in it. Maybe that's why Rivers hadn't called me? Maybe he's got The Pride? I checked the drawer in the bedside cabinet— empty…then the safe—it was open and empty. If the cops were in the elevator, I only had seconds left to find the stone and bail.

CHAPTER THIRTEEN

I SUDDENLY REMEMBERED the smuggler's hole—Kozzi's R. M Williams boots. I pulled them off him one at a time, checked inside them, and found The Pride wrapped in toilet paper in the toe of his left boot. On my way to the door, I stopped and bid farewell to my friend.

"Onya mate!"

I peeked around the door into the hallway—the coast was clear. But then I heard another ding. This time it had to be the cops. Like a fleeting phantom, I hoofed it along the corridor in the opposite direction of the elevators, in a beeline for the emergency exit. I reached it just as voices of people entering the corridor from the elevator became clear enough for me to recognise Santana. Now it was me on the run from the cops as well as Rivers or whoever had murdered Kovacs.

I reached the car and sat behind the wheel, thinking. With my new passport and The Pride, the job was done. All I needed to do was get to the airport and hop the flight to Sydney Kozzi was supposed to take. But there was something more important eating at my guts—whoever had killed Kozzi needed to pay for it, and I wasn't convinced Santana would nail the bastard. It wasn't that I didn't have faith in him—I just figured the murder of a foreigner could easily go cold unless someone was there to drive the investigation. The Australian Consulate would be useless, and there were no known relatives of poor old Kozzi, so it was up to me to get square.

It was also obvious there was a mole amongst the cops; otherwise, the killer wouldn't have known when it was safe to hit Kozzi. As I figured it, there were only two choices: check into another hotel or see if I can stay at Malika's place for a bit. With her close ties to Al Head and Lexi, I felt the latter option was fraught with danger, but that disadvantage could well be turned to an advantage by keeping close to the pulse. I had to risk telling her the truth and chance her calling Al, Lexi, or Rivers to give me up. For Kozzi's sake, I decided to give Malika a try and drove out of the Andaz Hotel for Hillcrest.

~ ~ ~

It was just after lunch, and I hadn't eaten, so I stopped at the Canyon Country Store on Laurel Canyon for a quick bite. Sitting in the Mustang in the car park, I phoned Gary in Australia and gave him the bad news about Kozzi and the good news about having the stone. He took it badly, worried for my safety. He wanted me to leave immediately for Sydney. I promised to call him back once I'd sorted out a few things. There wasn't much more I could say, really.

There were outdoor tables at the Country Store, so I found a seat and ordered a Reuben sandwich and a coffee from the waitress. Man, when it turned up, it was the biggest sandwich I've ever seen. As well, the waitress kept refilling my cup until I was so wired I couldn't drink another drop.

"That's one heck of a sandwich," I said to the waitress, as a conversation opener.

"Oh, you'll finish it alright. Is that an English accent?"

"No, Australian."

"Oh, way cool, you're an Aussie then?"

I liked the idea of my nationality putting me on the Hollywood cool list.

"Are you in showbiz?" she asked with a cute smile.

She was the archetypal Californian beach girl, shoulder-length platinum blonde hair, blue eyes, an hourglass figure, lovely legs jutting out from a short, faded denim skirt—a cute package complete with a sort of vagueness that the uninitiated could easily mistake for naivety.

"Yes. I'm in film finance. You?"

"Well, of course I'm an actress, just about every blonde female in Hollywood is an actress, but at least I can say I was born here."

"Yeah, you look Californian to me. Tell me, is there a telephone here? I need to make a call."

"A phone? You've gotta be kidding ... everyone's got a smartphone these days, so, no."

"I see."

"Anyhow, nice to meet you Crocodile Dundee," she said with an adorable giggle.

"She'll be right, mate," I replied with the broadest Aussie accent I could muster, which got me an even cuter snigger.

As I watched her lovely tanned legs and rounded bottom disappear back inside the store, I was content I had proof that Lexi couldn't possibly have made a call to Malika from the Country Store. She'd left her cellphone at home, so she must have been with the murderer. That meant Malika was supporting her false statement, and that cast serious doubt on her integrity, but it was a means for me to test if I was safe with her or not.

~ ~ ~

It was pushing 3 p.m. by the time I pulled up in the driveway of Malika's hacienda, wishing I had my best friend holstered at my hip.

I knocked on the door and after a moment, it opened to Dorris, the maid.

"Good afternoon, Mr Stone," she announced happily.

"Hey, Dorris, is your mistress in?"

"Miss del Mundo? Yes, of course, follow me, please."

She led me poolside and offered me a chair at a table shaded by a large umbrella.

"I will inform Miss that you are here, sir."

After a few minutes, Dorris returned.

"Miss is coming, sir... Can I bring you a drink?"

"Yes, a JD on the rocks would hit the spot, thanks Dorris."

Malika floated out onto the patio like an angel. Underneath the flimsy see-through white chiffon wrap cloaking her shapely body, I could see the outline of a tiny string bikini... She was ravishing. I clambered to my feet.

She kissed me ever so gently on the lips.

"Hello darlink, back so soon?"

I pulled a tight face. "I need to talk with you about something very important."

"Sit down... You look so serious, darlink. Is everything all right?"

We sat. Dorris brought our drinks and then retired inside.

"No, everything isn't all right..." I went on to tell her the complete story, watching her eyes like a hawk for the slightest hint of deception—but only sighted shock, horror, and genuine concern for the death of my friend Kovacs. When I'd finished, she called Dorris and ordered us doubles. By her expression, she wasn't quite sure what to say about my allegations.

"You're right, Axis, I did cover for Lexi about ze Country Store. She was brought here by two men, one of zem tall and skinny with a face like a rato, is that how you call it?"

"A rat?"

"Yes, a rat, and ze other looking like a bodybuilder. They brought her to ze front door, den she told zem to leave. I only kept her secret because of ze police."

I was expecting the description to be of Sonny Rivers. I queried, "Did she say who they were?"

"No, only zat she had called zem to bring her here. She didn't want to call me because it could have meant trouble for me if I came to ze crime scene."

"I see, so she had her cellphone with her?"

"Yes."

I shook my head slowly, "Another lie from Lexi... it's not looking good for her. What did she tell you about the murder?"

"Ze same as she told you... ze fight with Carson—she was hiding upstairs—he would hit her ven he got angry, you know? It wasn't ze first time she had come running here after a fight... anyhow, zen she heard shots and immediately phoned Al."

"So, Al must have either arranged those men to pick her up and bring her here, or they were the killers."

"Perhaps... I'm sorry for lying to you, Axis," she gently took my hand, "but I thought it was only a little white lie... and besides, zat was before we—" She finished the sentence with a sad warm smile.

"The last thing I want to do is place you in danger, baby. Right now, I'm on the run from Al, the cops, and whoever murdered Kovacs. I've got nowhere to hide—"

"You're not an American citizen, so it will be difficult for ze cops to find you, no? As for Al... well, I must tell you, Lexi called me last night, and ven I mentioned zat we had made love, she went ballistic. So, you're probably safe here for now. We just need to get rid of your car."

I wasn't impressed that she had told Lexi, but some women are like that. I let it go.

"It's an Avis..."

"Give me ze keys. I will have Maurice return it."

"Maurice?"

"My gardener and handyman," she said softly. "But I think you should consider speaking with dis detective because ze last thing you need is to make an enemy of ze police. You know in zis town they have ze reputation of shooting first and asking question later."

I loved the way she often left the plural off her words. "Yeah, that bothers me too. But you're right, I better set up a secret meeting with him."

"Why secret?"

"Because I'm not convinced his lieutenant is on the level... he has a rat face. He might be the mole I suspect. Hmm, if the Mustang is going back, I'll need wheels."

"Come with me, darlink," she said with a cheeky grin.

She led me by the hand through the inside connecting door to the big double garage. Parked there was a current model silver SUV Mercedes and a late-model orange BMW Z4 Roadster. The Beamer was looking happening until she took me to the front of the two cars and lifted a tarpaulin off a brand spanking new Harley Davidson Road Glide Ultra.

"Will zis do?" she said with a twinkle in her eye.

She knew exactly what turns on a bloke like me.

"Don't tell me you ride this?" I exclaimed.

"No, no, no. It belong to a French boyfriend I had. I kick him out because he owe me so much money... but I kept his bike. Zat's enough about dat. As far as I know, it has only been rode a few times."

"Ridden," I corrected her.

"Yes, ridden... Can you ride?"

"Is the Pope a Catholic?" I said.

Her brow furrowed, perplexed. "Yes, he is, of course..."

"Sorry, it was just an expression. Yes, I can ride."

I checked the odometer; it showed only eighty-five miles.

"It has hardly done any work. What a beauty."

"I thought it would be best because in ze black leathers and helmet, you won't be recognise."

She held up a key ring. "Bike and the front door key."

I took it. "What is the third key for?"

"Perhaps zat is ze key to my heart? You will find out later. Shall we have something to eat?"

She took my hand and led me back inside the house. I couldn't help wondering where she got all her money. A big sprawling hacienda in the Hollywood Hills, three hundred grand at least in cars, dripping with jewellery, a maid, a gardener—the life of Riley, no less.

"I guess you wonder vere I get all zis," she said, as though she had read my mind.

"I must admit I am."

107

"Two very favourable divorce settlements and several big-budget movies playing supporting lead roles. Come."

She led me into her den. A clap of her hands triggered the lights. Three of the walls were decorated with framed movie posters, awards, and photographs of her with famous actors, directors, and producers. The fourth wall was stacked with books, and right in the middle of them, commanding pride of place, was a metre square nude portrait of her, looking absolutely exquisite.

"What a stunning painting," I uttered.

"Zank you, it was done last year by ze same artist who painted Naomi Watts. She is also Australian, no?"

"Born in England and moved to Sydney when she was fourteen or fifteen, got into acting and moved here. Her father was the road manager for the British progressive rock band Pink Floyd. You know them?"

"Yes, I love zem. Come on, let us not dwell here... I become self-conscious showing off my achievements."

My eyes were drawn to her beautiful figure. "Your achievements look fine to me."

She blushed.

"When did you move here?" I continued.

On the way out, she clapped her hands, and the lights turned off.

"Nice trick," I observed with a chuckle.

She led me back through the living room out onto the patio poolside. We sat in deck chairs, and she called Dorris to order food and coffee. Then she carried on.

"My first husband is ze owner of a small bank in Rio. He brought me here six years ago ven I was only twenty-two. We'd only been married three month. He co-financed a big Hollywood action movie you might remember called Conquistador?"

"Yes, with Antonio Banderas."

"Yes, and also another Australian, Eric Bana. I had a small part but it was enough to get me noticed by a producer. We had a little affair and zat led to a divorce and a new marriage to ze producer, his name was Carson Kincade ... now do you get ze picture?"

That I hadn't expected. "Ah, right, so that's how you know Lexi?"

"Yes, Carson and I only lasted two years. He couldn't perform, if you know vat I mean. He just like nubile young girls and little boys. I got co-lead in one movie with him called Programmed to Kill. I played Carmen, and ze part launched me to stardom. Zere was a young French actor on ze movie I had a fling with... it was his Harley Davidson. At ze same time, Carson met gold digger Lexi, and an amicable divorce follow."

"So, you two stayed friends?"

"Me and Lexi? No, no, no... just six months ago, Carson call me to try and talk me into doing another movie with him. I didn't realise at ze time dat it was just a ploy to use my name to get funding so he could guarantee Lexi a part in it... and, of course, Carson wanted to produce it. I didn't want to know about it. I'd had enough of him."

"Uh-huh, and the film was Wait Until Dark."

"Yes, zat's vat all zis is about, no? Ze opal and everything, and now your poor friend... how was he killed?"

"Two bullets in the head, execution-style... the same as Kincade: a professional hit."

"And who do you zink was ze killer?"

"I'm sure Al Head has something to do with it."

"I am not surprised, really," she said slowly.

"What makes you say that?"

"I met him through Lexi. She brought him to convince me to be in ze movie, but I said no, especially after a friend in ze business zat I trust advised me to steer clear of it. He told me Al Head was nothing but a cheap Vegas gangster. I knew Lexi must have a relationship with him. Zey know each other from way back."

"Who is your friend? Maybe he can help me."

"Yes, good idea. He has a lot of influence in Hollywood. His name is Gerry Mansfield."

"The film financier?"

"Yes, do you know him?"

"No, but Kovacs did... He originally met Kincade and Lexi at one of Mansfield's parties."

"Yes, zat would be right. It was me who took Lexi and Kincade to zat party. I might have even met Kovacs zere, but I don't remember."

"Okay, it's all beginning to make sense."

"I will call Gerry after lunch and ask him to drop by. He lives nearby on Doheny."

CHAPTER FOURTEEN

A LITTLE LATER that afternoon, after a few laps in Malika's pool, I was about to climb out of the water when I noticed a beautiful pair of sandaled feet standing at the edge. Recognising them immediately, I gave the toes a gentle, sensual lick with my tongue.

"Oh, don't do that, darlink. I am on ze way to a meeting. Gerry is coming at six for a drink. I have told Dorris not to mention to anyone zat you are here. Was zat right?"

"Thank you, my love. I don't know what I'd do without you," I said, and then reared out of the water, growling like a killer crocodile as I playfully chased her into the garage, leaving a trail of water in my wake.

We stood beside the Beamer and we kissed passionately. She whispered in my ear, "Now look vat you have gone and done, darlink. You smeared my lipstick."

When I got back to the pool, there was a JD on the rocks waiting on the table. I had to pinch myself to make sure I hadn't died and gone to heaven. If this is how the space that life occupies life in Hollywood is, then I'm the perfect fit.

~ ~ ~

After a shower and a change of clothes, I discovered Santana's business card in my pants pocket. I stared at it for a moment and then concluded that Malika was right—I needed to avoid making an enemy of the law—and so I called him.

"Carlos, it's Axis Stone."

He growled back, "Glad you rang. I've got half the goddamned cops in LA out looking for you."

"Yeah, sorry about that. You probably already know from the hotel CCTV footage that I found Kovacs' body just before you arrived."

"Yeah, I saw you sneaking along the corridor. I'm sorry you lost your friend."

"I had to get away and think. You understand that, don't you?" I appealed honestly.

"I do. It was a hit," he said grimly.

"Yep, same MO as Kincade."

"But with one major difference."

"What's that?"

"I've got them on CCTV."

"A positive ID?" I said excitedly.

"Not yet. I've got the geeks in forensics working on it, but I'm hopeful," he admitted.

"We need to talk, but I've gotta stay low. I'm not leaving the country until whoever hit Kovacs pays for it."

He sighed. "Yeah, I figured as much. Nice switch you pulled with the new passport."

"I'll explain that one when I see you. How about we meet alone at the Country Store on Laurel Canyon?"

"Okay, but it will have to be for breakfast tomorrow, say 7 a.m. I'm tied up today. You keep your head down now."

"I'll do my best. You've got my cell number, but keep it to yourself. Make sure Slim doesn't know we're communicating ... I've got good reason to be suspicious of him."

It was set ... I could now relax, knowing Santana would meet me in the morning. Now I could concentrate on building a profile on Al Head and Outlaw. I was hoping the notorious Gerry Mansfield would be able to connect the mad array of confusing dots for me. Questions like, is Outlaw legit? Could they really have the remake rights of Wait Until Dark? The answers to those questions would go a long way in determining the integrity of Head and his organisation.

It had just gone 6 when Malika arrived home. She was in one helluva fluster. I figured her meeting hadn't gone well, but she didn't have time to discuss it because Gerry was on his way. She rushed into her bedroom to change. Fifteen minutes later, she re-emerged elegantly attired, calm, and demure as though nothing had happened. Such resolve was only to be admired.

The doorbell rang, and Dorris went to answer. She brought back a tall, immaculately dressed, debonair, middle-aged gentleman.

"Gerry," Malika announced as she rushed over to give him a peck on each cheek, European style.

His greying hair was swept back, giving him an aristocratic Richard Gere in his forties look. With an ascetic face, he held out a hand for me to shake.

"You must be Axis. Pleased to meet you. Gerry Mansfield."

His voice was deep with a slight European accent, maybe Northern Italian? But his name gave no indication of his heritage.

"Mind if I call you Gerry?" I asked courteously, mentally noting the solid gold Patek Philippe watch on his right wrist.

"Absolutely, now Malika, where is that bottle of single malt Scotch you keep for me, dear?"

"In ze bar with your name on it, darlink. Sit down, and I will have Dorris pour you two fingers on ze rocks. Would you like another JD, dearest?"

"Thank you, Malika," I said warmly.

I could tell our little overly friendly repartee had piqued Gerry's interest.

"An Aussie, Malika tells me. You don't happen to know Josh Kovacs, do you?"

"Yes, actually, we came here together." I went on to explain everything. Three drinks later, I'd brought him up to speed and determined he was probably gay or at least a switch-hitter—but nonetheless, one of the good guys.

"You don't look surprised, Gerry," I said.

"It really isn't uncommon here, darling. If I had a dollar for every movie scam I've seen pulled in this town over the last thirty years, I'd be a very rich man."

"But you are a very rich man, Gerry," Malika quipped.

He smiled devilishly. "Well, I guess I might have had a dollar or two in some of them," he chuckled.

"Can you answer this for me," I asked in all seriousness, "could Al Head and Outlaw own the remake rights for Wait Until Dark?"

"Well ... now that's a real interesting question. The rights came up a few years back when the writer died. Warners tried to exercise their option, but a consortium outbid them ... and I can tell you that consortium had nothing to do with Outlaw or Al Head. So, the answer to your question is no—unless, of course, he bought the rights from that consortium—and I assure you if that were the case, then one Gerry Mansfield here would know all about it."

"Okay, second question ... from your knowledge, is Outlaw a legitimate film production company?"

"Now that is a difficult one ... anyone can incorporate a company and call it a film production company. There would be literally thousands of them in Hollywood alone. But I can tell you this much, darling ... to my knowledge, Outlaw has not been involved in the production of a film here to date."

"Okay, then maybe if I rephrase the question ... would there be any reason to suspect the probity of Al Head?"

"All I know about him is basically what Kincade told me when he asked me for a bridging loan. As soon as he mentioned the title of the project, I told him what I've just told you. I said I knew nothing of Outlaw and that I thought Al Head was probably a gangster... Somewhere along the line, I'd read something about him being involved in casino racketeering in Vegas. Kincade tried to sell me on how Head was worth millions and all the usual crap about how with his production expertise and Head's marketing prowess they were going to set the film world on fire. Then, when Malika asked me for a recommendation, I advised her to steer well clear of it and them."

"It was excellent advice, my dear friend," she said with an appreciative smile.

Gerry didn't stay much longer; he had a dinner appointment. But he had certainly cleared up a lot of my queries. After he'd gone, I was sitting by the pool with Malika, having a drink.

"I'm meeting Detective Santana at seven in the morning."

"I am so glad you called him. Does he have any problem with you fleeing ze crime scene?"

"It seems not. Anyhow, enough about me, what happened at your meeting today?"

"Oh, it vasn't a show business meeting, darlink. It was something quite different."

"Well, go on, I can see you're disturbed by it," I pressed.

She let go of my hand and wiped a single tear that had forced its way out from between her long eyelashes.

"I was with ze doctor. I have been diagnosed with breast cancer ... he wants to remove my left breast." The floodgates opened, and she broke down. I jumped up and took her in my arms.

"Oh baby, I'm so sorry. Shouldn't you get a second opinion?"

"Zis is ze fourth opinion, Axis," she groaned. "He said if zey don't remove it quickly, it is likely to metastasize."

"Oh baby," I hugged her and let her cry for a moment, patting her on the back, the way my mother did when I was a pup. Eventually, she calmed down, pulled back, and peered at me through watery eyes.

"What do you think I should do, darlink?"

"I'll help you get through it, love."

Her eyes again flooded with tears. "Would you really do zat for me, Axis?"

"I promise. Look, if I get through all of this, find Kovacs' murderer, and get the opal back to its rightful owner, I will be here for you."

"I wish I had met you earlier. You are such a special person, Axis."

I looked into her eyes and felt the urge to expose my inner self to her, something I definitely wasn't in the habit of doing with anyone.

"Look, I can be a lot of things, many of them not so good—"

"Don't worry, darling... no need to—"

"Let me finish, baby... I can be self-centred, obnoxious, arrogant... some have called me misogynistic or narcissistic even ... but you, Malika, you make the world make sense to me, and that has never happened to me before with any woman. You bring out the best in me."

Tears had welled up in her eyes. We kissed, deep and passionate.

She looked me in the eyes, "You have enough on your plate darlink, without my problems."

"I've survived too many storms to be bothered by raindrops, love. I'm in the here now with you."

She sniffled, then said, "Show me ze opal, darlink."

I was a little taken aback. After my confession, I thought she would've wanted me to explain more about myself, but no. "The opal?" I questioned... it felt like a reprieve. "Sure, okay, just give me a minute."

I went to the guestroom, sat on the bed, took off my boot, and retrieved the stone from inside the toe. Then I returned and placed the opal in her open palm. It shone radiantly red and green in the light.

"Oh my God, it is so beautiful! You say it is worth a quarter of a million dollars?"

"Yes, it's called The Pride."

"Do opals have healing properties?" she asked.

"I don't know, maybe. Are you into that sort of thing?"

She took an iPad from the side table and Googled.

"Yes, I believe in ze powers of ze mind, spirit, and ze planets. Zis is vat it says: traditionally, in crystal healing, opal has been considered good for headaches, eyesight, Parkinson's disease, blood, insulin regulation, PMS, and ze immune system. Wow, zat's pretty good. I should meditate with it on my breast tonight."

"And me with it."

With her eyes once again sparkling she said, "Darlink, can I ask you serious question?"

"Sure, go ahead."

"Why do you do vat you do ven it is so terribly dangerous?"

"I guess it's rusted on. Originally, I planned to be an author like my dad was, but well, I suppose life got in the way."

"Did you ever write anything?"

"Yes, I started on a book but never finished it."

"Vat is zis book called, darlink?"

"A place beyond forever."

"Zat is a beautiful title."

~ ~ ~

I was up bright and early the next morning. Malika gave me a set of black leathers and a helmet that seemed tailor-made for me. Within minutes, I was garbed up and ready to take on the Harley. Considering it had been standing for a long time, I was amazed it started at the press of a button. Lacking confidence, I wheeled it out of the garage, gave Malika a kiss goodbye, put on the helmet, hopped on, and then unsteadily motored down the driveway onto Hillcrest. It took me only a few minutes to regain my riding confidence, and then I totally got off on the rush of the corners and bends on Laurel Canyon Drive.

The Canyon Country Store was up ahead ... it had just gone 7 a.m. I rolled into the car park, and as I got off the bike, I saw Santana seated at a table reading the LA Times. As I walked towards him, I had a hollow feeling in my gut and wondered if it was because I was missing Malika.

CHAPTER FIFTEEN

❝THE LAST THING I expected was for you to turn up in leathers," Santana taunted, casually folding up the tabloid.

I peeled my gloves off, shook his hand, and then sat down opposite.

"You people have it lucky here, the weather is always the bees-knees."

"Oh, I don't know," he growled, gazing up at the azure blue sky. "I grew up in East LA, where we hardly saw the sky," he chuckled.

We ordered breakfast and coffees up front.

"Good coffee here," I said.

"You mean this café or California?"

"The Country Store."

"So, you've been here before?"

"Yep, and they don't have a phone," I said dully.

"A phone? Why is that significant?"

"Lexi Diamond said in her statement that she called her friend from here at midnight, but there's no phone, and the place closes at eleven on weekdays. She said she'd left her cellphone at the crime scene."

"Aha," he lounged back in his chair, chewing on a toothpick. "Go on."

"She lied, and someone gave her a lift to her friend's home, but who?"

"Yep, a fair question... what else have you got?"

"Someone must have told the murderer where and when to hit Kovacs," I grated.

"Why's that?"

"Because there was only a small window of opportunity between me giving him the opal and you guys arriving to escort us to the airport, and none of the likely suspects knew Kovacs was staying at the Andaz, let alone in that room."

"Feasible. So, do you suspect Lexi Diamond? Before you answer, tell me this: why kill Kovacs?"

"Hear me out," I urged. "The room was turned over looking for the opal; they must have known Kovacs had it."

"What are you driving at? Spit it out, son," he growled uneasily.

"Slim Williams is from Vegas."

"Ah, I see where you're going. You think because Williams is from Vegas, he might be on Head's payroll and tipped off the murderer. You'll need more than that, son."

I shrugged. "What if he and the murderer accompanied Lexi Diamond to her friend Malika's place after they'd knocked off Kincade?"

"Any proof?"

"Malika described Williams to a tee — he took Lexi to her front door. My hunch is when Kovacs and I got involved in the whole shebang, it caused complications for Williams and his relationship with Head. Tell me, who came up with the idea of running us out of town?"

"Williams," he groaned.

His expression was beginning to show acceptance of my hypothesis.

"Williams is the mole. No doubt about it," I growled.

"Okay, I'll level with you, son," he said. "Williams has been under suspicion for a while now. He was transferred here for a reason."

"Did they know in Vegas he was on the take from Head?"

"Yeah, something like that."

Our food arrived.

"Figured as much — any luck with the CCTV?" I quizzed.

"A little, there were two of them. We got a reasonable ID on one, Anderson Volt ... a known gunman from back east. But the face of the other guy was obscured."

"Who's in charge of running down Volt?"

"Williams."

"That might be a conflict of interest, dead in the water for sure," I said facetiously.

"Why the hell are you still in town anyway? You obviously got what you came here for, what's the use of hanging around? You'll only get your goddamned head blown off—"

"You're right, I've got the opal, but there's still a score to settle. Look, someone hired Volt to murder my friend, and in my book, that person needs to be dealt with."

"Johnny Cash once waxed lyrically: I shot a man just to see him die," Santana chuckled.

"Folsom Prison... one of his best. Look, what you do for yourself dies with you, but what you do for others lasts forever."

"I like the way you think, Stone," he admitted.

"Thanks."

"All right, now listen-up... I want Head's ass as much as you ... I want Volt, his accomplice ... and I want to nail Williams, but I've got no jurisdiction in Nevada, and the cops up there can't be trusted ... too many on the take. The only decent cop I knew there was the guy who had Williams transferred down here on suspicion for me to deal with ... now that guy is six feet under — two bullets in the back of his head. He left behind a wife and three little kids. The Williams corruption deal is how this whole goddamned thing got started, but instead of getting it sorted out, it got damned worse."

"Why?"

"Because Williams is only the tip of an iceberg."

"How about Sonny Rivers?"

"That cheap jackass Vegas crook ... one of Head's henchmen, you've obviously met him?"

"Yup, he did the deal with me for the opal."

I thought it prudent to leave out Kovacs masquerading as Mr Stein the jeweller and the scam we'd pulled on Rivers to win back the opal. Santana didn't ask, so I didn't offer it up.

"We've had eyes on Rivers for a while. You know he's one of the leading suspects in the Kincade case? I wouldn't mind betting he was Volt's accomplice in the Kovacs killing; the other guy in the CCTV. I ordered him brought in for questioning, but he's blown town, presumably to Vegas. What about Kincade's widow, Lexi Diamond?" Santana asked.

"She's with Head in Vegas. I think she bailed out because she'd conspired to set her husband up for Head."

"Yep, I agree ... I came to the same conclusion, but why?"

"Probably something as lame as a part in Head's movie."

"Incidentally, I reported the murder of Kovacs to the Australian Embassy ... it's standard procedure ... they sent a messenger around this morning to collect his personal effects. So, where's the opal?"

I unzipped the side pocket of my jacket, pulled out the stone, and handed it to him.

"Ooo wee, now that would make one heck of a bolo-side!" After relishing it, he reluctantly handed it back. "I could keep it, you know?" he said with a cheeky, single raised eyebrow.

"I guess you could, but we both know it belongs to someone else."

He took a sip of coffee and eyeballed me over the rim of the cup. "I won't ask how you got it," he rasped with a wry smile.

I carefully changed the subject. "Nice eggs Benedict."

"Yep, they do a good one here, not up to Denny's standard but certainly palatable," he chuckled, wiping his moustache with a napkin. His expression suddenly changed to serious. "Now here's what I propose, use this phone..."

By the time I climbed onto the bike to head back to Malika's place, we had formulated an audacious plan. I had his full support ... and to confirm it, he'd slipped me an unregistered Smith and Wesson model 6904, nine-millimetre handgun. I hadn't used the model before, so he pointed out its benefits of being compact and easy to conceal. It felt good to have a piece again.

~ ~ ~

The ride back to Malika's place was swift and exhilarating, evoking a sense of rejuvenation and recapturing my youth. I found Malika near the pool, engrossed in a phone conversation. Immediately, she gestured for me to be quiet, indicating that she was talking to Lexi. After concluding the call, we shared a kiss.

"Was that who I think it was?" I inquired warmly.

"Yes, I've been on ze damn phone with her for ze past hour," she complained.

Taking a seat in the chair opposite her, I asked, "What did she want?"

"You won't believe zis, but she's still trying to sell me on zat stupid film," Malika replied.

"You can't trust anything that comes out of her mouth, kiddo. Did she ask about me?"

"Yes, I told her I haven't heard from you. I asked her ven she would be back in town, and she said not for a while. She wants me to visit Al's ranch in Nevada. I said no way. Why do you think she still hassles me about zat film?"

"I guess they're desperate for a big name to attract more investors and rip off. With Santana confirming what Gerry Mansfield had said, you shouldn't go anywhere near Al Head," I cautioned.

"If zat means keeping away from him, den yes, I will. Let's have a drink, darlink. I'm tired of talking about zose imbeciles."

An hour later, I received a call from Williams and walked out to the garage to have a conversation away from Malika. He requested a meeting to discuss the schedule, but in reality, there was nothing to discuss—it was Williams making a move. I contacted Santana.

"Carlos... Axis, Williams took the bait. He wants to meet up tonight," I informed him.

"That was fast. I only gave him the carrot an hour ago. They must really want your ass, real bad," Santana replied.

"More likely the opal," I speculated.

"I hear you. Have you set a time?" Santana inquired.

"No, I told him I'd text him one. I have his number," I explained.

"Good. I'm going to activate an app on the phone I gave you to relay audio. Now listen carefully ... wear the phone in an outside pocket. Will you be wearing the leather jacket you wore today?" Santana asked.

"Yes," I confirmed.

"Good, put it in the zip pocket you took the opal from, got me?" Santana directed.

"How observant of you," I remarked.

"That's my gig. The cell coverage is fine for a radius of fifty miles, so we won't lose you. We'll not only be listening to your every word and his, but tracking you as well," Santana assured me.

"Good," I acknowledged.

"It's best to talk with him in his car—we've got it bugged as well and tracked as backup. I'll have a chopper and uniforms mobilised. You know what to do with the gun, right?" Santana inquired further.

"Sure. So, I'll meet him at the Canyon Country Store in an hour," I confirmed.

"Good thinking ... okay, my friend, best of damn luck," Santana wished me.

That was it—I was on my own, and the challenge left me completely buzzed. I sent Williams a text, arranging to meet him at the Canyon Country Store in an hour, then returned indoors to prepare.

While I was dressing, Malika entered the guest room and caught sight of me concealing the gun.

"Are you going out?" she asked curtly.

"Yes, I have to meet someone. I should be back in a couple of hours," I replied.

She embraced me, her voice filled with concern. "Axis, I saw ze gun. Why? I don't like zis," she protested tearfully. "You could get yourself killed."

I held her close, looking deep into her beautiful eyes. "Malika baby, this is what I do. I'm a private detective."

"Zat doesn't mean I have to like it. Vot if something happens to you?" she expressed anxiously.

I handed her Santana's card. "Here, if you don't hear from me by midnight, call Carlos. He'll know what to do."

"Carlos?" she questioned.

"Oh, sorry. I'll call him Carlos after the legendary guitarist Carlos Santana," I clarified.

We shared a passionate kiss. As she pulled away, her Latin temper started to boil.

"You give me strength, Axis. I don't vont to lose you now. I zink I am falling for you," she confessed.

"Hey, to be honest, I'm feeling something for you I've never felt before as well." I kissed her passionately once again.

CHAPTER SIXTEEN

I PULLED THE bike into the car park of Canyon Country Store on time. There was no sign of Williams, so I took a table and ordered a coffee, deciding to wait. The night hour was quite pleasant, with car headlights flashing past on Laurel Canyon Drive. The warm air carried a strong scent of eucalyptus, reminding me of home. In 1919, Californians planted many Australian Eucalyptus trees in the Hollywood Hills to stabilise the eroding soil. These trees thrived in the climate due to their low water requirements. However, Australians know from experience that eucalyptus oil, which gives the trees their characteristic fragrance, is highly flammable. When combined with dry, windy weather and leaf litter, it can turn a small ground fire into a terrifying firestorm in minutes. As I recalled the Black Sunday bushfires, a late model black Toyota RAV4 pulled into the car park and flashed its lights. Assuming it was Williams, I quickly finished my coffee and made my way toward the car. As I reached the front passenger-side door, it swung open and I climbed in.

"Sorry I'm late," Williams said stiffly.

"That's okay, I enjoyed a coffee while waiting," I replied.

I immediately sensed someone behind me, but before I could turn around, I felt the cold steel of a gun barrel pressed firmly against the back of my head. I stiffened, berating myself for not being more cautious.

"Two shots in the back of the head is your practice, isn't it, Volt?" I said icily, deducing the identity of the person behind the gun.

"So well informed, Stone," Williams responded mockingly.

I realised immediately that with Volt present, Williams would have to eliminate me to protect his secret. Now, I had to put my faith in Santana's plan.

"Miracle intuition, it's called, Slim. Though I wouldn't expect a man of your limited IQ to understand that," I retorted.

The lights suddenly went out.

~ ~ ~

Gradually, my surroundings came back into focus. First, a dull thumping headache accompanied by an ache in the pit of my stomach. A quick assessment revealed that Volt had hit me over the back of my head with his gun, rendering me unconscious. It felt too cold, and I realised I had been stripped down to my underpants and boots. In the darkness, I could make out that I was seated in a chair, my hands tied behind my back and ankles secured to the front legs. My leather jacket was missing, along with the phone it contained. This dashed any hopes of Santana coming to my rescue. However, there was still a glimmer of hope—Santana had bugged Slim's car.

As my eyes adjusted to the darkness, I noticed a sliver of light under the door. The air smelled of oil, indicating that I was likely in a vehicle workshop. The approaching footsteps warned me of an impending visitor. The door swung open, flooding the room with light, temporarily blinding me. A flickering fluorescent light above revealed the surroundings—a definite auto workshop. I had guessed correctly. Through the haze of my throbbing head, the rat-faced Williams came into focus.

"Ah, if it isn't my favourite bent cop. Did you secure a role in Al's movie as well?" I remarked.

"You have a big mouth for someone in your position, Stone. I might have to cut out your tongue to shut you up ... after you tell me what I want to know," Williams threatened.

"That's not the kind of incentive that would work, Slim. Didn't they teach you anything about being a criminal at the police academy? Besides, you're not the type to get your hands dirty so don't flatter yourself. If it were your buddy Anderson Volt threatening me, I'd be trembling in my boots," I taunted.

"I can arrange that... Oh, about your not-so-smart phone with Santana's tracking and monitoring app, Anderson is taking it for a ride. So, you're on your own, mate. That's what you Aussies call each other, isn't it? Mate?" Williams sneered.

"Again, you flatter yourself, Slim. You're no mate of mine. In fact, you're probably no mate of anyone," I retorted.

"Once my mate Volt gets back here, you'll be meeting your maker unless you tell me the whereabouts of the opal," he threatened.

"And then what?" I challenged.

"That's up to someone else," he replied, looking down at me with like I was an allergy.

"There's no point in telling you where it is because only I can access it," I growled.

He began pacing the floor, clearly frustrated. I was successfully getting under his skin, which was my intention.

"So, kill me, cut out my tongue, do whatever you want, but none of it will get you the opal. And I don't think Uncle Al will be too happy about that, will he? You know, when I first saw you, I thought you looked like a praying mantis. Now, in this light, I'm certain you are one," I provoked.

He snapped and lunged at me like a man possessed. He delivered half a dozen heavy slaps across my face, causing my lips to split and my nose to bleed. Panting, he stepped back to assess his handiwork.

"Now look at what you've done, Slim. I'm getting blood on my nice, clean undies," I spat, expelling a clot of congealed blood onto the floor.

"Where is it, Stone?" he shouted.

"You must have a screw loose. Why would I tell you?" I defiantly replied.

He struck me again, and this time, a few stars danced before my eyes.

"Talk, or I'll break your fingers one by one," he threatened.

"I refuse to engage in a battle of wits with an unarmed man," I grumbled.

He raised his fist, ready to strike once more.

"Look, it's simple. I've hidden it in a safe place that only I can access. You'll have to take me there to get it," I revealed.

He got in my face. "Yeah, where's that?"

"The safe in my hotel room. And of course, only I know the combination," I disclosed.

"What hotel?" he demanded.

"You're not a very good cop, are you, Slim? You should know details like that. Geez, I hope Volt hasn't taken off in your nice RAV4," I goaded him.

"He'll be back... What hotel, Stone?" he insisted.

"Which hotel would be better English. I figured if it was good enough for John Belushi and Jim Morrison, then it would be good enough for me—the Chateau Marmont," I revealed.

He stormed out, slamming the door behind him. At least he left the light on. While I was glad the beating was over, I didn't particularly care about my phone being taken for a ride by Volt. As long as he used Slim's RAV4, Santana would be able to track it. I hoped Santana would quickly decipher what had transpired.

It didn't take long before Slim returned.

"Alright, you're going to take us to your hotel and hand over the opal," he commanded.

"What makes you think I'd do that?" I challenged.

"If you want to keep your face recognisable, you'd better drop the wise-cracks," he warned.

A hulking figure loomed behind him.

"We haven't been formally introduced, but I assume you're Anderson Volt? The one who murdered Carson Kincade and Josh Kovacs," I gritted through my teeth.

Standing at six feet four inches with a spiky blond crew cut and a strong square jaw, he resembled Major Chip Hazard from the movie "Small Soldiers."

"Does Tommy Lee Jones do your voice-overs?" I quipped, but it seemed to go over his head.

Then, a hand the size of a keeper's mitt crashed across the side of my skull, knocking me senseless. The blow made me realise that it was time to ease up on the sarcasm.

Williams untied me, helped me get dressed, and guided me out of the room while pressing the barrel of his gun into my ribs. It was dark, and there wasn't much to see as they quickly bundled me into the backseat of the RAV4. Williams sat beside me, ensuring that I had a clear view of the 9mm Glockmeister aimed at my gut. I needed to continue my rhetoric to ensure Santana could record the conversation and stay one step ahead of us.

"Well, here we are, Slim, Volt, and Stone... sounds like the name of a hardware store," I mumbled groggily.

"Shut up, Stone," Williams snapped.

"Tell me, what happens once we've been to my hotel room and I've handed over the opal? What are Big Al's orders? Two bullets to the back of the head, I suppose," I said, purposefully revealing the information for Santana.

"You'll find out soon enough," Williams replied, his tone curt.

It suddenly dawned on me that something was different about the RAV4— it wasn't Slim's car!

Curious, I asked, "Why aren't you driving, Slim?"

"Because Volt doesn't like anyone else driving his car," Williams deadpanned.

I had relied on our plan going according to script, but now it seemed that everything was falling apart. The cavalry wasn't going to arrive. While Santana would know that Williams would be taking me to my hotel room, he needed to know the exact timing to synchronize the rescue and make the arrest. My phone was gone, and we weren't in the bugged car. A wave of queasiness washed over me, and I sank a little lower in my seat.

Chateau Marmont loomed in the night sky over Sunset Boulevard, its Gothic spires casting eerie shadows. It reminded me of a misplaced Bavarian castle that had been transported through time.

Williams parked near the entrance, and they both escorted me into the lobby. It was close to 1 a.m., and the reception was devoid of human activity, except for the night porter catching some shut-eye. With the Glock pressed into my left kidney, I led them to the elevator—a spectacular sight with its ornate facade that almost resembled an opal. The entire decor and trimmings of the hotel were beautifully Art Deco. This was old Hollywood at its finest, with just as many live-in ghosts as the Hotel California, and I had no intention of joining their ranks.

My room was on the fifth floor. We reached the door, and I took out the key card from my pocket. "I bet you're glad there's no CCTV," I quipped.

The absence of CCTV was precisely why Santana had suggested this hotel. It ensured that Williams wouldn't wait in the car, leaving Volt to carry out his part of the plan. We needed to apprehend Williams; his accomplice was secondary.

"This place gives me the creeps," Volt grumbled.

"Ah, the creature speaks!" I exclaimed, opening the door to my room.

"Put a sock in it, Stone!" Slim growled, jabbing the Glock harder into my back.

The sensor lights illuminated the room as I led them inside. It consisted of a bedroom, bathroom, and living room—old-fashioned but cosy.

Volt walked over to the sliding glass windows, opened them, and stepped out onto the small balcony to take in the view.

I turned and faced Williams. "They said Johnny Depp stayed in this room last week."

"Thrilling. Now, get the damn opal!" Williams growled, pointing the pistol at the bedroom door.

He followed me inside. I needed to act quickly while Volt was still on the balcony. I rushed to the wardrobe, opened it, and punched the code into the safe. Williams kept the gun barrel pressed against my ribs.

"No funny stuff, or you'll end up dead," he snarled.

I stopped just short of entering the last digit.

"How could there be any funny stuff? I'm unarmed and not in my own country. Can you move back a bit so I can see?" I requested, locking in the final digit. He gave me some room. I reached inside the safe, withdrew the jewellery box, and tossed it to him. He fumbled to catch it and dropped it.

"Be careful. Al wouldn't want it in pieces," I cautioned.

As he bent down to pick it up, I slipped my hand behind into the safe and withdrew the 9 mil Carlos had given me. I fired two shots into Williams' chest. He went down. Volt came running and stopped in the doorway. I fired at him, a big enough target but under pressure I missed. He turned on his heels and took off. I went after him. He raced along the corridor faster than a bloke his size should be able to travel, and then he disappeared through a door I figured was the fire escape. As I reached it I heard a loud click; he'd locked it from the other side. There was no point going after him, I raced back to the room and found Williams standing unsteadily holding his chest with one hand and his gun in the other bleeding all over the bedroom carpet. The gun trembled slightly as he raised it to shoot me but before he could get off a shot, he collapsed onto the floor, thank God. I walked over to his twitching body and put a courtesy slug into his forehead. Fuck him.

It wasn't long before the sound of rumbling feet and muttering arose in the corridor outside the room. The four gunshots had disturbed the other guests. I went to the phone, dialled Santana and told him to bring a body bag.

I picked up the jewellery box, opened it and chuckled at it being empty, Williams had died for an empty jewellery box worth about eight bucks — the opal was safe and sound at Malika's house.

The mini-bar called to me, so I grabbed a JD, flopped onto the lounge, and raised my glass in a toast to Slim Williams lying on the bedroom floor in a sea of blood.

I snarled, "One down."

CHAPTER SEVENTEEN

S ANTANA CRUISED INTO the hotel room with his characteristic swagger. I was surprised to see him alone. I raised my glass and said in my best cowboy accent, "Howdy partner, pity we failed to put the wagons in a circle."

Chewing on a matchstick, he reached into the side pocket of his brown tweed sports jacket, pulled out my phone, and tossed it to me. Juggling my JD in one hand, I managed to catch it.

"At least you got your phone back ... still working, by the way," he remarked.

He went over to the body sprawled out on the bedroom floor and knelt down beside it.

"Two shots in the chest and one in the head ... headshot from close range. You better give me your piece before I bring in the uniforms."

"You want a statement?" I asked.

"No, I know Volt's MO when I see it," he mumbled, punctuating his words with a wink.

I handed him my gun, and he quickly wiped it clean of fingerprints.

"This is the murder weapon. I'd say Volt was wearing gloves when he did the damage, left the gun, and then took off. There won't be any prints," he glanced at me sceptically.

"Yeah, sure," I stammered. "Maybe mine when I picked it up and went after him."

Carlos knelt down beside the body. "Yep, Williams went down in the line of duty," he said, removing the Glock from Williams' right hand. He got up and handed it to me. "Use this now, it's a throw-down." He then reached back down, turned Williams onto his back, opened his coat, and removed the pistol from his shoulder holster. "This is his police weapon."

He placed it in Williams' right hand, completing his ruse. We returned to the lounge room and sat down.

A faint sheen of sweat had formed on his forehead. He pulled out a handkerchief, wiped it away, and sighed. "Okay, I'll fill you in on what happened here. We hadn't counted on Williams leaving his car on Kirkwood Drive across from the Canyon Country Store and then riding in Volt's vehicle. So much for technology ... give me an old-fashioned wire any day."

"I'm with you on that one. I guess it would have been smarter for me to know the make of Williams' car," I admitted.

"Yeah, well, we're often smarter in hindsight, aren't we? So, back to the story ... you met Williams here to discuss an exit strategy that I had briefed him on earlier. You were discussing the MO when Volt burst into the room with a gun. He didn't expect you to have company, especially a cop. Williams drew his weapon, but Volt fired first and put two slugs into his chest. You rushed into the bathroom and locked the door. You heard another shot, came out, found Williams on the floor, picked up the pistol, and took off after Volt, but he had already fled. Got it?"

"No sweat," I replied.

"Good. Your face tells a story you can tell me later." He got up, went to the door, and let the uniforms waiting outside come in. Within minutes, the room was teeming with them.

Santana's demeanour had changed to match the occasion. "You'll have to stay in town a bit longer, Mr Stone. There will be an inquiry into the officer's death. For now, you'll accompany me to the station to make a statement."

He drove me to the Canyon Country Store, where I retrieved my bike, and then followed his car to the Beverly Hills Police Station.

~ ~ ~

By the time I left the police station, it was dawn. I hopped on my bike and headed to Malika's place. Santana and I had agreed to meet up later in the day to discuss the next move, designed to implicate Al Head. The capture of Volt would be left to the police, and I was more than happy about that. The guy frightened the crap out of me. Al Head was another matter—we both knew he had orchestrated the murders and needed to be brought to justice. However, while he was in Nevada, his ranch provided him with sanctuary, keeping him out of the reach of the law.

I was looking forward to getting a couple of hours of sleep, maybe even some action with the beautiful Malika to relieve the tension. However, my thoughts shifted to her problem, which made my own dreams seem insignificant. With the breeze rustling through my helmet, I sped along Sunset Boulevard, flooded with thoughts of the special connection I had found with Malika, unlike anything I had experienced with any other woman. I wondered if this feeling could be love. No, it couldn't be. Could it? But the anticipation of seeing her gave me butterflies in my stomach—a tell-tale sign, perhaps. Right then, the billboards flicked past, reminding me that I was in Hollywood, and I couldn't have asked for anything better. As I passed Chateau Marmont, illuminated by the sunrise, reality struck, and the butterflies flew away. I had killed a man there just a few hours ago. The act wouldn't be written into Hollywood legend, but from my perspective, there was no denying that it had happened. I had condemned a new ghost to roam the hallowed corridors of Chateau Marmont at the witching hour.

~ ~ ~

With birds chirping and the sun shining, I parked in the driveway of Malika's hacienda. Dorris wouldn't be at work yet; she usually clocked in at 10 a.m. Leaving my bike and helmet behind, I went inside to open the garage. Malika had given me a key to the front door but not the remote for the garage door. Trying my best to be quiet so as not to wake her, I gently eased open the front door. However, a light left on in the living room caught my attention, preventing me from proceeding to the garage. I walked through the house and down the split-level into the living room, where I turned off the light. Something felt off—a few things were out of place, items overturned, broken glass on the floor, a discarded robe, and a single slipper. Untidiness was not one of Malika's characteristics. Then I noticed that the underwater swimming pool light had been left on.

Treading cautiously, I went through the open glass doors onto the patio and froze at the sight before me. A naked woman floated face down in the pool, surrounded by a ghastly red stain. My mind was screaming this can't be Malika. Without hesitation, I dived into the water and took her in my arms. Like a man possessed, I rescued her, gently lifting her out of the pool and onto the poolside. I climbed out myself and rolled her over, laying her face up. I was repulsed by the terror frozen on her face. Her right eye socket was a bloody empty hole, and her throat had been brutally slashed, revealing the spine in the gaping wound. A hideous message had been carved into her chest, reading: "an eye for an eye."

As the meaning of the message sank in, I involuntarily let out a loud scream. It was Volt, that mongrel! Consumed by rage, hate, and a desperate need for revenge, I paced the poolside like an angry tiger, wringing my hands, feeling sick to my stomach. My mind raced with thoughts of how I could find and kill the bastard. But then, in a moment of clarity, I realised that nothing—absolutely nothing—would bring Malika back. I regained some semblance of rationality and reminded myself not to touch anything; this was now a crime scene. And that's when Santana came to mind. I reached for my phone, my hands trembling, and dialled his number.

~ ~ ~

Sitting by the pool, my head in my hands, I slowly glanced up at Santana. This time he wasn't alone - a veritable army of uniforms had accompanied him and were pouring all over the place. After a quick check of the body, he took me by the arm and walked me out of the house, away from the throng. We got into his car and drove off.

~ ~ ~

We found a table in a quiet part of Denny's. I was staring out of the big tinted windows transfixed on the traffic outside on Sunset, thinking of how in the space of an hour the magic of Hollywood had soured, when Santana's voice broke my reverie, his voice filled with genuine concern. "Are you with me, Axis?"

I looked at him, still lost in my thoughts. "Yes, I guess so, mate," I mumbled, my voice barely audible as I ended with a dispirited sigh.

He sighed deeply, his eyes filled with understanding. "She meant a lot to you, didn't she?"

I fought back more tears. "The first time I've felt that much for a woman in ... I don't know, a helluva long time, I suppose. She had breast cancer, you know? We were working on getting her an operation. I was going to stay in L.A. with her." A tear trickled down my cheek. "You know what makes it worse?" I confided, my voice filled with a mix of sorrow and anger.

Santana nodded, his expression sombre. "Volt must have gone directly from Chateau Marmont to murder her."

"I'd say he was ordered to do it, son. He's a pro, not the type to act spontaneously or do it as a personal vendetta, even though he left his calling card. I'd say it was a message from Al Head," Santana replied, his voice filled with understanding.

"Yep, I suppose you're right... it was a contract killing," I growled, anger overriding my remorse. From the look on Santana's face, he could read it.

"You'll need to keep a grip on it, son. The chance for revenge will come, but it needs to be well thought through," he cautioned.

"I know, I know... but can you get Volt?" I asked, my voice laced with desperation.

"He'll slip up, don't worry. They all do eventually," Santana reassured me.

I glared at him, knowing deep down he was right. "But how many more have to die before that happens?" I questioned, my frustration mounting.

"You and I both know who's next on the hit list."

"What are you thinking?" I rasped, my mind still chaotic with emotional turmoil.

"I'm running out of options, Axis," Santana admitted with a heavy sigh.

I shot him a determined gaze. "What do you want me to do?"

At that moment, nothing would please me more than to invite Anderson Volt into my space so I could exact my own version of an eye for an eye.

"We'll need Malika's phone," he said, dialling on his own phone. "Murphy. Have you found the victim's cellphone? Good, get a uniform to drop it off at Denny's on Sunset pronto."

We were on our second cup of coffee when a uniformed officer arrived, delivering Malika's phone. Santana immediately began surfing the call log.

"Lexi called her at ten thirty last night."

I was taken aback. "That's just after I left to meet Williams. What do you make of that?"

Santana leaned back in his chair, pondering the question. "Hmm, maybe Malika said something to her about you, and that prompted Al Head to send Volt to silence her. Did Lexi know you were staying there?"

"No, Malika knew not to mention it."

"Hmm, I put a record order on Malika's phone yesterday. Give me a second," Santana said, dialling the Special Communications Division of the LAPD to arrange for the sound file to be sent to him.

After a sip of coffee, he put his phone down and said, "Comms will have it in a few minutes."

"I didn't know you could do that."

"Well, officially I can't. It's inadmissible as evidence in court unless obtained through legal means. But the new anti-terrorist laws provide a loophole."

His phone buzzed, and he put it on speaker so we could both listen. The voice on the recording was Lexi's.

"Malika, it's Lexi," she said.

But it wasn't Malika's voice at the other end. "No, Miss Lexi, it is Dorris. Miss Lexi can't come to the phone right now; she is outside with Sir."

"Outside with who?" Lexi asked, her tone brash.

"Sir Axis, he is going for a meeting."

"Oh, so Sir is staying there?" Lexi inquired.

"Yes, ma'am. Shall I tell Miss Malika to call you? No?"

An irritated Lexi snapped, "No, no. I'll try again tomorrow. Just tell her I called."

The call ended, and Santana placed the phone on the table. "Is Dorris the maid?" he asked.

"Yes, and she unwittingly gave me away."

"Apparently, when Dorris arrived for work today and learned what had happened to Malika, she passed out and has been taken to the hospital."

I nodded, understandingly. "Poor thing must have been devastated."

Santana looked at me, aware of the anguish etched on my face. "You need to get some rest, buddy. Come on," he said, gesturing for me to follow him.

Together, we set off to a police safe house in Santa Monica, hoping that a change of environment would bring some semblance of peace amid the chaos that surrounded us.

~ ~ ~

As I sat on the sofa in the living room, the first light of dawn filtering through the window, I stared at the gun in my hand. Sleep had eluded me, my mind and emotions in turmoil. Losing two people close to me in as many days was taking its toll.

"Hey," Santana's voice startled me, causing me to almost drop the pistol. "Whoa! Put that down... Tough night, huh?" he said, concern evident in his tone.

"Sorry, man. Yeah, my mind's full of turmoil."

"Only to be expected, son. Go take a shower. We'll meet Lieutenant Murphy at Starbucks nearby in an hour or so."

~ ~ ~

I watched as a tall, thin young guy with a pleasant face, swept-back hair, and long sideburns entered Starbucks. He joined us at our table. I knew it had to be Murphy because he was carrying my port.

"Sir," he announced with veneration of his superior officer.

"Pull up a chair, Murphy. This is Axis Stone, he's an Aussie PI," Santana introduced.

Murphy shook my hand, handed me the port, and then sat. Murphy looked a lot like Harry Callahan, the cop made famous by Clint Eastwood in Dirty Harry. His vibe implied he'd graduated from the school of hard knocks.

"Lieutenant Murphy is up to speed, Axis. Now, by my reckoning, we won't be hearing from Volt again. By now, he's probably in Mexico or Rio. But you keep an eye out, Murphy, in case we get a lead. In the meantime, Stone and I will focus on Al Head ... I've got no doubt he's behind this entire caper."

Malika's phone rang in my pocket. I drew it and checked the caller ID. "It's Lexi Diamond on Malika's phone."

Santana held up a warning hand. "Let it ring out. She might leave a text when there's no answer."

"Tells us she can't know Malika has been murdered," I said.

Santana took a bite of banana bread. "Hmm, maybe."

The phone signalled an incoming text. I read it out.

"Mali, keep this secret coz Al sez no-one's to know—the ranch address is 6034 Olympia Hills near Southern Highlands Golf Club. Let's surprise him. Text your ETA. Lexi."

"Yep," Santana rasped. "That confirms it, she doesn't know Malika is dead."

We all paused to think about the text. Then I sat forward and said, "I'll take Malika's place and visit the ranch."

The look on Santana's face soured. "Like hell you will," he said acidly. "I'm not about to sanction an execution."

"So, I haven't told you then. Look, I'm just going to pay them a friendly visit. You told me yourself you've got no jurisdiction in Nevada. The local cops there are a risk, and Head's not going to turn up here. What choice have we got but to bring the bastard down in his own backyard?"

"We don't know what kind of support he's got there, for Christ's sake. For starters, Sonny Rivers, then maybe Volt, and probably an army of henchmen. You'd be walking into a death trap."

"If he wanted me dead, it would have happened by now," I argued. "He wants the opal."

"What opal?" Murphy bleated in surprise.

"Don't worry, son. I'll fill you in later," Santana said in a perfunctory manner.

"Maybe we should call in the Feds?" Murphy added.

Santana reacted glibly. "No, they'd just mess things up. Get yourself a coffee, son."

While Murphy went to the counter to order, Santana continued collusively. "Don't even think it, Stone."

I sat back and folded my arms defensively. "Your perception ain't bad for a guy nudging his use-by-date."

"Don't start that crap, the gold watch will fit me just fine."

I unfurled my arms and leaned closer to him. "What we need is someone who can put together a task force to chopper into the ranch to take him and his cronies out. I know it's illegal, but you and I also know it's what needs to be done ... and I know just the guy." I pulled out my phone, ready to dial.

"Wait, son. Talk it through first. Don't be so Goddamned impulsive."

I complied and pocketed my phone.

"So, what's this about?" Carlos asked.

"I know this guy Nick Vargas, a millionaire. He got me this case, and he has limitless resources. Basically, anything money can buy, including a small army of mercenaries. I know he'll help ... he has connections here."

Murphy returned with a coffee. "Did I hear right?" he said, taking his seat, astounded. "You're going to assemble an illegal army to attack this guy's ranch?"

After a pregnant pause, a smile creased Santana's craggy face. "You had me going there for a minute, Stone."

I knew he wanted to keep it from Murphy and so bought into the gag.

"Guess I've been in Hollywood too long. Sounds like the plot of a Steven Seagal flick, doesn't it?"

~ ~ ~

We watched Murphy drive out of the Starbucks parking lot. As we got to Santana's Ford Explorer, he said sternly, "We need to talk."

We got into the car.

"I can't fathom how you can just let a murderer walk," I complained.

"You're talking about Bolt? Let me tell you, son, when it comes to a domestic murder, it's pretty straightforward. Either the perp eventually gives himself up, or he spills the beans to someone who blows the whistle on him. Nine times out of ten, we only have to wait for it to unfold by itself. But contract killings are a totally different animal. Assholes like Bolt have an exit strategy in place well ahead of the hit. It's premeditated murder. The odds are in his favour."

"I get that. So Murphy might be right. If you can't get help from the Nevada cops, how about the FBI?"

"Been there, done that. If we take that option, then you might as well give up now. We'd lose control of the case, and the outcome would be an each-way bet. Besides, Head will have friends in high places."

I knew he was right, but it was only making me more frustrated.

We locked eyes. "That only leaves one option."

"That's why we're talking, son. You serious about this guy, Vargas?"

"Damn right I am."

"My involvement would be off the record. You know that, don't you?"

"Absolutely," I agreed.

Santana's mood had changed. He was now in positive mode and said with a touch of excitement in his tone, "I've got some boys who'd be willing to enlist for a raid on this scumbag."

"Cops?"

"Former Nevada cops with a score to settle with Head but with no support to do it legally."

"Friends of the cop you said had been hit?"

"Yeah, the one that left three kids and a wife ... my sister," he growled with contempt.

I was shocked. "Your sister?"

"I left that part out. The cop killed by Head was my brother-in-law," he confided.

I stared long and hard into the eyes of my Latino friend, with the knowledge he had more than enough reason to bring down Head.

"How many?"

"Two pros plus me."

"What about Murphy?"

"I'll put him onto finding Volt. That'll keep him occupied. He's a good young cop, but he doesn't have the grounds for retribution we do."

"Cool." It made sense. "In the meantime, I'll base myself at Malika's house ... can you clear that for me?"

"Done ... anything else?" Santana agreed, offering his hand to shake. "Partners?"

"You betcha!" I replied, shaking his hand.

CHAPTER EIGHTEEN

I WAS STANDING on the driveway of Malika's house, feeling like a shag on a rock as I watched the CSI forensics team depart. Being back at the house meant facing the harsh reality of Malika's murder, and it left me feeling uncomfortably numb.

I wandered back inside and found Dorris, who had returned from the hospital. I explained that I would be staying there for a while and assured her that I would continue to pay her wages. She wiped away her tears and bravely got back to work.

I lowered myself into a deckchair beside the pool, but the water, still stained with Malika's blood, left a hollow feeling in my gut. I pulled out my phone, ready to call Nick, but as I looked at the pool, my thoughts were consumed by the image of beautiful Malika floating face down in the crimson water. I got up, went to the bar, poured myself a stiff JD, threw it down, poured a second one, and took it back poolside, hoping it would provide enough Dutch courage to face my demons. I grabbed my phone and dialled.

"Mr. Nick Vargas, Axis, yeah, I'm alive. I've got a situation, man. Gary told you. No, I don't want to discuss it over the phone. I'll text you the details. Okay, cool, later."

I sat on the deckchair and started typing a text. Suddenly, a voice from behind startled me.

"Sir, there was a message from the family of Miss del Mundo."

I pressed send and turned around. "Oh yeah, what did they say?"

"There is no father or mother, only a younger sister and brother of Miss," she said, barely getting the words out before breaking down in tears. I quickly got up and helped her take a seat.

"Hush now, Dorris, it's all right... please go on," I comforted her.

She wiped her eyes and blew her nose on a handkerchief. "I be alright ... is terrible shock, sir. Her brother Brandon is 17. He at school in London, and Malika pay his fees, you know? He is good boy, studying to be actor like his sister."

"So, it was the sister who left the message then?" I asked.

"No, sir, the brother."

"Okay, go on."

"The sister, Beleza, I know her from before... she visit here once. She only a little younger than Malika. She arrive today from Rio."

"Here? She arrives today? What?" I yelped, taken aback. I wasn't expecting that.

"Yes, sir. She arrange de funeral and everything."

That threw a spanner in the works. "Okay, okay," I stammered. "The sister, Beleza, that's fine. Um, you better stay here to introduce me, otherwise it might be awkward."

Nodding her head with a sullen expression, Dorris got up. "No problema, sir. I be here. You like lunch?"

I wasn't particularly hungry, but I figured making me something might take Dorris' mind off things. "Yes, a sandwich and coffee would be great, thank you Dorris. Tell me, if Malika means Queen in Spanish, what does Beleza mean?"

"It mean beauty, sir. Beleza is beautiful, just like Miss."

I sat down with my mind boggling at the prospect of meeting a woman as beautiful as the most beautiful woman I'd ever met. Beleza, I repeated to myself. The word seemed to roll musically off the tongue. 'The Terrible Tango' broke my reverie; it was Nick.

"Nick. Excellent, you're on, great."

He had spoken to a friend in Arizona who agreed to loan him his Bell 407GXP chopper. He asked about weapons, and I told him Santana would handle all of that.

"I'll meet our ex-Navy SEAL friend, Dan, at LAX and then come to you. He's flying in from Hong Kong," Nick said.

"Whoa! Just wait a second, buddy ... I didn't expect you to come. This'll be dangerous."

"Since when does danger stand in the way of a good adventure? Besides, I've got a vested interest to watch over your fat butt and my buddy's three-million-dollar chopper."

"I hear you," I replied. "I'm not about to argue. I've got a base here; I'll pick you up from LAX."

"Not necessary, just text me the address. I know my way around L.A. We'll come to you. See you tomorrow, amigo."

I sat back with the warm sun on my face, contemplating what a great friend I had in Nick. Dorris arrived with a tray, and I tucked into the baloney sandwich, an acquired taste from my time in America, and poured myself a mug of coffee.

I must have nodded off after eating because Dorris woke me when she was removing the tray.

"Sorry, sir, I didn't mean to—"

"It's okay, Dorris," I reassured her, sitting up and knuckling my eyes. "How long have I been asleep?" I asked, bleary-eyed.

"Two hours, sir."

It was a typical Californian summer's day, which meant a swim was definitely in order. I went to my room, slipped on my swimmers, returned, and dove into the pool. The filter had done its job by then and finally cleared the water. After a few laps, feeling refreshed, I was just about to start another lap when I heard 'The Terrible Tango'. I hopped out of the pool quickly and answered.

"Hello? Hello?"

"Axis ... Santana. Did you get some rest?" he asked.

I lowered myself into a chair under an umbrella. "Oh, a couple of hours. How about you?"

"Ah, no, too much damned paperwork," he grumbled.

"I've got most of what we discussed arranged. My people will arrive tomorrow."

"How many?" he inquired.

"Two, but there's a hitch," I warned. "Malika's sister is arriving any minute from Rio to take care of the funeral arrangements and the estate."

"I know ... the lawyer handling the estate has already called me."

"What's his name? I should speak to him," I said casually.

"He's a celebrity entertainment lawyer, Gerry Mansfield."

"I know him. I'll give him a call."

"Be careful what you tell him. This is a small town built on big rumours."

"I hear you. Let's set up a meeting when my guys arrive."

"Okay, call me ... and listen, just because we think Volt has left, don't drop your guard. Anything could happen with that cunning bastard on the loose."

"Copy that."

The call left a bad taste in my mouth. Would Volt be able to track me here? I doubted it. But still, I needed to watch my back as Santana had warned. I phoned Mansfield.

"Gerry, it's Axis Stone. Yes, terrible, isn't it? I found her in the pool." I got up and paced about. "I don't know, but the police think it might be connected to the Kincade murder. Yes, Dorris told me she's arriving here soon ... I'm at the house. I'll leave all that to her ... I'll only be in town for a couple more days, then back to Oz. She what? Now, why would she go and do that? Oh, I see. Okay, let me talk it over with her when she arrives. Ciao."

"Hello, what are you doing here?"

The voice startled me. I turned expecting to see Malika standing there. It was her voice, same accent, same intonation — same lovely warm texture with a slight hint of humour. But standing before me wasn't Malika ... it was an angel. My knees almost buckled at her heavenly appearance.

"You must be Beleza?" I stammered.

"Yes, and I still don't know why you are here. Are you cleaning ze pool?"

"Yes, no," I babbled, flustered. "Please, sit. Let me explain."

After an hour of explanation, she seemed satisfied.

"Does zat mean I am in danger being here, Mr Stone?"

"Please, call me Axis. Look, I can't say you're not in danger, but what I will say is I will be staying in the States until I get the guy who murdered your sister."

"Zat is very heroic of you, Axis, and I'm sure your intentions are valid. But it seems crazy to me zat you would risk your life to avenge ze murder of a person you knew for less zan a week."

"The time I was fortunate enough to spend with your sister means more to me than any other time in my life," I assured her genuinely. "She was a very special lady, and nothing will stop me from avenging her murder."

"Seems personal."

"It is, and a whole lot more. At the risk of it sounding like a line from a Hollywood action film, animals like Anderson Volt, Sonny Rivers, and Al Head can't be let get away with taking your sister from us."

"You know vat, Axis? I believe you. But did you not know Malika was dying?"

The words hit me like a ton of bricks. "No, no ... um, it can't be ... I mean, I didn't ... I ... I knew she had breast cancer but—"

She cut me off. "The breast cancer had metastasized into her lymph nodes. She had been given six months, six months ago."

I bowed my face into my hands. It was all beginning to make sense. Gerry had told me Malika had left me something in her will. She must have known. But why didn't she tell me?

"I can tell by your reaction you're probably wondering why she hadn't told you?"

I looked up at her through teary eyes. "Yes, exactly."

"I think I'm ze only person, other zan Gerry Mansfield, to know. She was probably going to tell you eventually. Don't feel bad, Axis. I think you must have been very special to her; otherwise, she wouldn't have told Gerry to write you into her will."

"I don't want ... but wait a minute, that means she knew she was going to die?"

"Listen to me ... you must accept whatever she wanted to give you. My sister was a great judge of character. When she loved, she loved with a passion. Zat is how she lived her life, zat is why she was a great actress, and zat is how she would want to be remembered."

She reached across from her chair and gently took my hand.

"Honor her by accepting her gift of love," she continued warmly. "Because vat she couldn't give you in life, she has given you in death."

We embraced, and the scent of her body, identical to Malika's, caused me to nuzzle her black hair, just as I had done with Malika. We both wept.

After a few compassionate moments, she held me at arm's length, gazing deep into my eyes, and said crisply, "Whatever you plan to do in seeking revenge for ze death of my sister, I will be doing it alongside you. Because I have an even greater right zan you for vengeance. Do you understand zat, Axis?"

It took me a moment to answer. The sheer grit and determination in her words assured me she wasn't going to back down, no matter what I said.

"Can you handle a gun and shoot to kill?" I asked.

She nodded sharply. "Yes."

"Then I agree in principle, but not entirely until I can say I know and can trust you. So, it's not final, okay?"

She fired me a cheeky smirk. "So, first I need to win your trust, huh?"

"Yes, Beleza, you do."

"I have no problem with zat."

She had that same lovely cadence as Malika, with her English pronunciation.

She stood up and asked softly, "In which room do you stay?"

"The guest-room."

"I will take Malika's room."

"Are you sure?" I was concerned she might not have known it was where Malika had met her fate.

With a sincere smile, she affirmed, "I know she died in zat room. I am comfortable with zat."

She called Dorris and ordered her bags to be taken to Malika's room and unpacked. In the same way as her big sister, she took control, and I loved it. While she was busy moving in, I slipped back into the pool for a few more laps.

~ ~ ~

I didn't see Beleza until Dorris called us to dinner just after sunset. She floated into the dining room as if on a cloud. Dressed in a shimmering silver wrap-around evening gown that hung loosely at the front to display the cleavage of her beautiful, full, high breasts, she looked exquisite. The designer had created the full-length dress to showcase her hourglass figure, and the thigh-high slit allowed her beautifully shaped legs to emerge when she walked, revealing her stunning sandaled feet. With her hair up and her light brown skin glowing in the soft amber glimmer of dusk, she was a sight to behold. Luckily, I had decided to dress formally for the occasion and looked quite dapper in a tailor-made suit. We gazed at each other, breathless, for a few minutes until Dorris broke the silence.

"I serve you apéritif?" she said with grace.

Beleza's lovely almond-shaped blue eyes twinkled. "I brought Champagne. It is being chilled. Would you care for a glass, Axis?"

"Yes, but I warn you, bubbly has been known to make me do unpredictable things."

"Good, zen bring ze bottle and two flutes with ze aperitif, Dorris."

We sat in wicker armchairs, facing each other.

"So, I will begin my education on all I need to know about the beautiful Beleza del Mundo."

"And she will do her very best to tell you only vat she wants you to know about her," she said cheekily.

"You are so much like your sister. Are you an actress?"

"No."

"Do you have a boyfriend?"

"I have suitors, but a boyfriend, no."

"Why have you stayed in Rio when you could have lived in Hollywood?"

"I have been finishing my Master of Arts at ze Federal University of Rio de Janeiro."

"Do you like me?"

"I like you as much now as I did ven you were in your swimsuit."

I took that as a positive. Dorris arrived with the aperitifs—a bottle of French bubbly, an ice bucket, and two Champagne flutes. I took over the task of uncorking the bottle.

CHAPTER NINETEEN

T HE CORK FROM the second bottle of Dom Pérignon sailed across the room and ricocheted off the terracotta floor tiles to our wild, inebriated cheers. Dorris appeared and announced dinner would be served in five minutes. The first bottle of champagne had loosened our tongues, which meant we were now custodians of many personal truths about one another. Nothing I had gleaned had altered my regard for her. I only hoped the same could be said of my confessions. I topped up our flutes—hers overflowed— and she quickly siphoned off the bubbly brew through her sensual lips.

"Well done, hardly dripped a drop or dropped a drip ... did that come out right? Think I'm getting my worms mixed up," I joked, and that got a laugh from her.

"You were right about ze effect bubbly has on you. I'm beginning to get a little bit wobbly myself. Tell me, who is Axis Stone really? What was ze boy like?" Beleza inquired.

It wasn't my norm to open up about my life to strangers or anyone for that matter. However, under the circumstances, I felt compelled to break the rule.

"I'm just an ordinary working-class man by Australian standards. I was born in Sydney and taken by my folks to New York as a baby. I was raised there until the age of four when, after the tragic deaths, I was sent back to Sydney to be educated at a boarding school. After that, I was a bit of a knockabout until I joined a band. That didn't last long; they soon found a better guitarist. After that, I went to London, as pretty much all Aussies did in their early twenties. I joined a band there called World, recorded an album, then couldn't make ends meet. So I backpacked around Europe for a while and eventually went back to Sydney. I did it tough in the school of hard knocks there, then landed a job in security, which led me to branch out on my own."

"Why a PI?" she asked.

"Guess it runs in the blood. My mum and dad were a writing team; they wrote hard-boiled detective pulps."

"I'd like to hear your music," she said.

My mind flashed to "Foul Play," the song I'd recorded with World that underscored the argument I had with Sherri, the miraculous masseuse, to end that relationship.

"I'm sorry about your parents. What happened to them?" Beleza asked.

"Who?" I snapped out of my reverie.

"Your parents. Was it an accident?... I'm sorry, maybe I shouldn't have—"

She had detected my reluctance to talk about them.

"No, no, it's okay ... I just haven't talked about it to anyone before. The truth is, I don't know. The death certificates for both of them state the cause of death to be coronary, but I find that difficult to believe."

"Why?"

"Because they were both fitness fanatics."

"That does not mean—"

I had said enough and changed the subject.

"Come on, let's take our drinks to the table and feast on each other as much as the food," I suggested, taking her hand and helping her out of the chair. We went up the few steps to the mezzanine dining area, where we found the large mahogany dining table elegantly set for two. At the centre of it burned a three-branch silver candelabrum. The main lighting was low, so the flickering candles embellished the romantic ambiance. I selected background music, which immediately drew a comment.

"Barry White's 'Can't Get Enough' album. Do you have a penchant for music of dat era?" Beleza asked.

I grinned. "Let's just say I have a sentimental attachment to most things of that time. You could say I'm mentally stuck in the '60s and '70s, sometimes the '80s."

"Those were romantic times. The music personifies zis ... times when air travel was an adventure, women smoked cigarettes, men pulled out ze chair for ze lady to sit, opened ze car door for zem. Manners, Mr Stone, something zat has sadly gone missing to be replaced by arrogance and perceived political correctness. But you, Axis Stone, you are ze exception."

We dined on three courses, beginning with lobster bisque, followed by a chargrilled swordfish cutlet, and then the pièce de résistance for dessert: vanilla cherry soufflé. As Dorris was serving the soufflé, I complimented her.

"You've excelled yourself, Dorris. I didn't realise you were such an excellent cook."

"Uh uh, not me, no sir. I order take-out from Lucques, Miss Malika's favourite French-Mediterranean restaurant."

"Oh, well done all the same. The soufflé was to die for," I said.

The doorbell sounded, and Dorris went to answer. I had briefed her to be careful. She returned with Gerry Mansfield.

"Well, look at you two ... Am I interrupting a romantic interlude?" he said warmly.

Beleza rose and welcomed him with open arms; they embraced.

"Lovely to see you again, Gerry."

"I wish it was under different circumstances, Bella," he said with compassion. "I'm so sorry for your loss. I think we both have a broken heart."

We shook hands.

"Good to see you again, Axis."

"Sit down, Gerry. How about a glass of champagne?" I offered graciously.

"I wouldn't say no," he said with a smile and took a seat at the dinner table.

"Dorris, bring another flute," Beleza ordered.

As expected, Gerry was dressed debonairly—a navy suit over a pale green polo. He unbuttoned his jacket and relaxed back in the chair.

Then his face tightened. "Sorry to raise this, Bella, but has there been anything further from the police?"

"About the murderer?" I questioned.

"Yes, Santana called me today and mentioned forensics had come back with a quandary or two, but he didn't elaborate."

"How's that?" I asked, a little baffled. "I presumed it was a laydown misère."

"Apparently, her throat had been cut post mortem. She actually died from a bullet that had entered under her chin."

Beleza jumped out of her seat. We rose respectfully.

"Please excuse me, gentlemen," she said politely but noticeably upset. "I must go to ze bathroom."

We watched her leave and then sat back down.

"I think the topic may have disturbed her," Mansfield admitted.

"No doubt, go on," I implored.

"Forensics could tell from the blood spatter in the room that she was standing on the bed when she was shot. If you're thinking sexual activity, there was none. After she was shot, she was later carried to the pool where her throat was cut post-mortem and the rest was done."

"I don't get it. Why cut her throat when she was already dead? Why was she standing on the bed, and why did the murderer shoot upwards under her chin, for Christ's sake?"

"I have no idea ... unless it was staged?" he admitted.

"Staged? What are you trying to say?"

The idea of voluntary assisted suicide rocked me because, in a strange way, it made a lot of sense.

"No ... it couldn't be?" I protested. "Why then would he remove her eye and carve the words 'an eye for an eye' in her chest?"

"Look at it from a different perspective. What if it was a mercy killing, and then someone else did the rest ... the mutilation?" Gerry proposed.

"Anything to support that hypothesis?"

"Only that she withdrew twenty thousand in cash the day before."

"That unusual?" I queried.

"For Malika, absolutely," he said confidently. "She was never one to wantonly blow money."

I leaned across the table and kept my voice down. "You know what bothers me?"

"No, what?"

"Beleza's reaction to it all ... if she's at all like her sister, then you'd expect her to be filled with explosive Latin passion, but I've seen precious little from her."

He frowned. "And that means?"

"I don't know. Maybe she knows something that she's not telling us? Did you know about Malika's medical condition?"

He reclined in his chair. "Yes ... I did," he reluctantly admitted.

"And that she only had months to live?"

"That is quite correct, less, in fact."

"So, you and Beleza were the only ones who knew this? Malika hadn't told me. In fact, she'd only admitted to having breast cancer and that a mastectomy had been recommended."

"No, it had gone way beyond that, Axis ... I expect she didn't tell you because she was afraid of frightening you off. You were probably her last hope for some comfort or, dare I say it ... love."

I slumped back in my chair and gazed at the ceiling, mentally shot to bits. Everything that had been so carefully pigeonholed had now completely flown the coop. One big question remained whizzing around in my mind: did this change anything? I needed to speak with Santana.

"She left the estate, cars, and four million dollars in bonds to her siblings," Gerry continued. "And she left you the Harley Davidson and half a million dollars cash."

"What?" I yelped, completely blown away. "Half a million dollars? ... Christ, I'd only known her a few days!"

He glared at me. "Which tells you something about her state of mind, does it not?"

It was making sense, but I wasn't enjoying it at all. "If you change the way you look at things, the things you look at will change," I mumbled.

"What's that?"

"Oh, just a saying I have that seems to fit with me having to change my perception."

"As I mentioned to you before, Axis, you cannot refuse zis gift. It is my sister's way of saying she loved you, even if it was for only a short while," Beleza stated as she re-joined us. Instead of resuming her seat, she remained standing at the head of the table with her blue eyes locked on mine. "Yes, you are right, Axis. You must change ze way you look at things, and zen ze things you look at will change. I know vat you must be thinking, and yes, she had arranged her own death. I suspect it had been arranged before she met you. It matters not zat her death was arranged, but why ze unholy mutilation of her body?" she questioned, discreetly crossing herself.

I could see tears welling up in her eyes, and right then, I realised that the grief I hadn't noticed had been contained. She was holding it all inside, trying to be responsible and strong. I didn't think it was the time or place for her to let go, so I got up and changed the subject.

"I don't know about you guys, but I could do with a stiff drink."

"I'll join you for one, but then I must be going," Gerry said.

"Let's sit in ze living room where it is more comfortable. I'll have vat you have, Axis," Beleza said.

I made the drinks while the others made themselves comfortable, and Dorris cleared the dining table.

I handed them their drinks and sat down with mine.

"Axis, do you think this is related to the murder of Carson Kincade?" Gerry asked candidly.

"Yes, I do. Is there anything more you can tell me about Kincade, Lexi, Al Head, or Sonny Rivers? Sometimes it doesn't matter how small a detail might be."

He pondered the thought, then confided, "All I know is that there are people with a lot of money invested with Al Head looking for a way out."

"Have they come to you for advice?" I asked.

"You could say that. I sent them to the police."

"So, you're talking recent?" I said.

"Yes, like today," he confirmed.

"Is zis Al Head ze man you suspect to be behind it all, Axis?" Beleza asked.

"I believe so."

There was a pregnant pause while we all contemplated the accusation. I wasn't expecting to divulge it to Mansfield because I wasn't yet sold on him being on my side. As it turned out, he spoke up first.

"I'd put my house on you being right about that, Axis, but be careful whom you take into your confidence. If I were you, that would also include the police," he warned.

"Do you know something I don't?" I questioned.

"Only that a gangster like Head will have influence everywhere," he cautioned.

"Did you choose the word 'gangster' for a particular reason?" I probed.

"We're talking Vegas here and probably a fifty-million-dollar-plus film investment scam that might only be in its infancy but gaining impetus. I've seen scams actually turn into legitimate movies, but never with blood money," he said gravely. He checked his wristwatch, downed his Scotch, and stood. "I better get going. Let me know if I can be of any further assistance, Axis, and Bella, you know I'm here for you. I'll look after all the legal business. I promised that to your sister. I think the insurance claim might be doubtful, though, so be prepared for that."

"I understand," she said with a grateful smile. They caressed.

I shook his hand, and then Beleza walked him to the front door. I went to the bar for a top-up, mulling over everything Mansfield had said. I sank back into the comfortable armchair and sipped my drink.

Beleza returned and announced warmly, "I'm going to bed now, Axis. I am very tired ... I think we learned a lot about each other tonight, don't you think so too?"

I stood up. "Yes, Bella, we did, and my opinion of you has grown."

"Thank you, Axis. I can say ze same of you."

She kissed me gently on each cheek, and then I watched her beautiful figure meld into the darkness of the corridor.

I strolled out onto the patio and dialled Santana.

"Carlos, Axis ... Am I disturbing you, mate?"

"No, I'm still at the office," he groaned. "But I'll have to leave soon before I nod off. What can I do for you, mate?"

The use of the word "mate" sounded funny coming from him.

"We had a visit from Gerry Mansfield tonight. He told me he has spoken to you."

"Yep, that's right. I expect you're interested in the forensic results?"

"Damn right I am, especially if they're pointing at voluntary assisted suicide."

"Yeah, well, that's surely how it's looking. You obviously know the story by now. What I can say is that it happens way too often here in Tinsel-Town," he admitted with a melancholy groan.

"A tortured metaphor ... But wouldn't that mean someone else mutilated her body?"

"It sure does, Axis, and that complicates things further at my end but changes nothing at yours," he explained. "Volt must've come there, found her dead, and did what he did. It just means I've gotta find another killer now. And remember what I told you about murder in this town? Well, I left out mercy killings, 'cause they're the goddamned toughest of all — ass-covering on a grand scale."

"So, you're convinced then?" I pressed.

"I believe so. She withdrew a shitload of cash the day before, must've been to pay someone to do the job. Probably didn't know exactly when it was going to happen ... that might explain why there was no suicide note and why she didn't give you an emotional goodbye that day."

"What if Volt took the note?"

"Possible, but I think not."

"All right, Carlos, go home and get yourself some shuteye."

"I'll do that for sure. Talk tomorrow."

He was right. It was beginning to add up, and Beleza was also right in that it really shouldn't matter who killed Malika but who had mutilated her body — and that bastard must have been Volt, on Head's orders. He had probably come to murder her anyway but found her conveniently dead.

"Sir, you want me to stay tonight?" Dorris said, startling me.

"Oh, Dorris, um, yes, thank you ... if you wouldn't mind."

"No problema, sir."

"Listen, before you go to bed, did you know Miss Malika was very sick?"

She looked at me glumly and then down at her feet as if she had been caught telling fibs.

"Yes, sir, I did."

I could see she wasn't comfortable being questioned about it while she was still in mourning. After my experience in the Philippines with the mourning process, I expected it wouldn't be any different for Dorris, being Mexican with the same Spanish roots. I decided not to pursue it any further.

"Okay, Dorris, thank you. It was a lovely dinner. Good night."

"Good night, sir," she said and then scurried off.

I poured a nightcap and took it with me to the guest room. Tonight, the few too many drinks I'd guzzled would at least ensure a decent night's sleep. I'd be further comforted by the security of the 9mm under my pillow.

CHAPTER TWENTY

THE SOUND OF splashing water woke me at 7 a.m. I wasn't sure if I had been dreaming or if my mind was suggesting a pre-breakfast swim, so I slipped on my swimmers, grabbed a towel, and made for the pool.

The source of the splashing became evident as soon as I entered the patio: Bella was doing laps.

At first, I didn't notice anything out of the ordinary, then it struck me that she was wearing only an orange swimming cap — she was skinny-dipping. I went to the edge of the pool and waited for her to notice me. I figured it would have been presumptuous to dive in with her. She stopped where I was standing and looked up at me with a big wet smile.

"Good morning, Axis. Are you coming in?" she asked.

"Are you coming out?" I replied.

"Yes," she grinned.

I collected her white towelling robe from the deckchair, and when I turned back, she was standing naked, dripping in all her glory. I feasted my eyes on her stunning body. I held open the robe, and she turned her back for me to fit it on her.

"Thank you," she whispered provocatively.

She turned around, removed the cap, and flicked her long black hair out to rest on her shoulders. "Your turn," she said with a cute smile.

I threw my towel onto the deckchair and dived into the water. After a few laps, I could see her sitting in the shade of the umbrella, watching me.

I stopped swimming and called out, "Can you tell Dorris to put the coffee on and—"

"It's on its way with croissants," she interrupted.

"Ah, what a wonder woman you are!"

I finished half a dozen more laps, then hopped out.

"How many sugars?" she purred.

"None, love. I'm sweet enough without."

"You Aussies are crazy," she chuckled.

Her arms came up and twined around my neck, pulling my head down until our lips met. Her mouth was open, and I could feel her tongue pushing against mine — sweet-tasting and warm. There was a hot, sensual passion in her kiss that would have singed the soul of an evangelist.

She purred in my ear, "Axis, I want you, but not here, and not yet." Then she put her hands against my chest and gently pushed me away.

I straightened up, my excitement deflated like a pricked balloon, and then flopped into a chair. She smiled cheekily and closed her robe. It was like the curtain closing at the cinema halfway through the best movie you've ever watched. I could hardly wait for the opening of the next session.

We managed to get through breakfast without any further incidents, and then we both retired to our respective rooms to shower and change.

When we met up on the patio a little later, Bella was wearing Gucci sunglasses and dressed in a chic grey business suit with an ostrich skin briefcase in her left hand. Nothing elaborate for me, I was in my work uniform: black jeans, a Pink Floyd T-shirt, and riding boots.

She stopped and posed for me like a catwalk model.

I complimented her, "You've got more gleaming facets than a brilliant-cut diamond, each one of them as lovely as the next."

"Well, thank you, Axis ... and you're a hunk."

"Where are you off to?" I inquired.

"A meeting with ze insurance company ... Malika was insured for two million dollars. If it is determined her death was assisted suicide, zey will quash ze claim like Gerry said."

"Need me along?"

"No, it is only a preliminary briefing. Ze real crunch will come with ze final police report and ze issuance of a death certificate from ze coroner. Can you keep up with vat ze police are thinking?"

"Sure, I'll be speaking with Detective Santana later on today."

She sidled up to me and delicately stroked the side of my freshly shaven face with her fingers.

"And vat else will you be doing today, darling?"

"Darling, hey? Hmm, that sounds promising. I'll be here waiting to hear from my friend arriving from Australia. The flight gets in about 3 p.m."

"You have hours to kill."

I purred suggestively, "Well, if you get back early enough, I've got a few ideas on how we could spend it."

She leaned down and kissed me lightly on the lips, her touch faint so as not to smear her red lipstick.

"I might just take you up on that," she whispered sexily.

"Are you driving?"

"Yes, I will take the Merc. I feel safe with such a big car around me. Bye, my precious."

"See you, gorgeous."

So much love-talk after only knowing each other a day, but it felt as though I had known her for years. I studied the provocative sway of her hips to the front door. She glanced charmingly back over her shoulder at me to make sure I was watching.

Dorris brought me a fresh pot of coffee. I filled my mug.

"Dorris, where is Maurice the gardener?"

She reacted to his name like it was a dark secret.

"Maurice? Oh, he finish up, sir."

"Uh? How come? He was still working here when he returned my rental car a few days ago."

"I don't know, sir. I think he go back to Mexico."

"I see, okay when you finish your duties, go home, phone me at sunset to see if you're needed tonight, but come in tomorrow morning as usual, okay?"

"Yes, sir ... but I not sure ... my sister, she in the hospital, and I must visit."

"Oh, okay, how long?"

"Don't know, sir."

"Did you tell Miss del Mundo?"

"Yes, she said no worry."

"Okay, well, thanks for everything, Dorris."

She nodded and then scurried away like she was afraid I was going to bite her. She wasn't comfortable discussing Maurice, and I wondered why, and then 'The Terrible Tango' sounded incoming.

"Hello, Axis Stone."

"Stone, Lieutenant Murphy here. Santana asked me to call to say Volt was spotted in a downtown bar last night."

I sat up sharply. The idea of Volt still being in town gave me the shivers.

"Is it a positive ID?"

"We got the CCTV footage an hour ago ... it's a positive ID, alright. I traced him entering the bar, then leaving, but I got nothing on a vehicle. I suspect he took a cab."

"That's a worry. You'd reckon he'd only stay in town for one reason."

"That's our read too ... want me to send uniforms to where you're staying?"

"No, I'm flying out to Sydney today," I lied.

"Okay, well, keep your eyes peeled. We think Volt might have the job of getting that opal back."

"No doubt about that. Thanks, Murphy. I'll catch you another time."

"Yeah, good luck Stone. Safe Trip."

The call had revived the threat that Volt was out to get me, and sooner rather than later. But how could he track me down? I had to hope there wasn't another leak. I thought, who knows I'm staying at Malika's place? Mansfield, Bella, Santana, Murphy, and Nick, that's all. I had to rule out Nick, Santana, Murphy, and Bella, but I couldn't totally eliminate Mansfield. Was he here last night to check if I was staying? Is he playing me and, in reality, in league with Head? No, if that were the case, Volt would have hit me last night. I was getting ahead of myself. I had no control over what Volt was planning — I shouldn't be trying to second-guess him. I needed to control my own fate, sit tight, and remain vigilant.

With the house empty, to distract myself, I decided to do a little snooping. It is, after all, in my DNA. I grabbed my mug of coffee and wandered into Malika's den.

When I clapped the light on, my heart skipped a beat. The nude painting of Malika was glaring at me like a ghost — the eyes staring right through me, giving me goose-bumps. I went around behind the antique desk, put my mug on the desktop, and sat in the high-back leather chair. Fingering through the few documents on the desktop, I found nothing of interest. But then, when I opened the four desk drawers one at a time, I noticed something odd. I removed the small top drawer completely from the desk and found a locked secret compartment at the back of it. A letter opener from the desktop should do the trick, so I tried it in the heart-shaped lock to lever it open but had no luck. Picking locks for some PIs goes with the license; however, it's never been my forte. Sitting back, staring at the lock, trying to think it open, I was suddenly struck by a memory that caused me to look sharply up at Malika staring down at me from the wall. It was as though she had spoken to me from the other side, "Perhaps it is ze key to my heart, you'll find out later." The words resonated in my mind, and then the penny dropped. I looked back at the keyhole ... yep, it was heart-shaped. I fumbled in my pocket for the bike and front door keys, along with that mysterious third key she had given me. I tried it in the lock, and it fitted ... a twist, and it opened. Inside were three diaries.

Malika had been a dedicated diarist. From what I could gather, she hadn't missed a day since she made her first journal entry the day she arrived in L.A. I was certain the diaries would make compelling reading from that first entry, but curiosity had gotten the better of me, so I opened diary three at the very last entry and found, to my surprise, a note to me.

"Being the brilliant detective you are, my love, you have found my diaries and I am no longer. Please read them and weep, my love, for they contain my pain, love, loss, and elation. They tell my version of the truth, and they do not let a good story get in the way of it, even though this is Hollywood. Let me first say, I love you, Axis. These last days of my life spent with you were some of the most wonderful days ever for me. Why, oh why, did you not come along sooner, my darling, before this darkness delivered my fate? I have chosen to leave you and this world because I can no longer live with the debilitating disease that is eating me away physically, mentally, and emotionally. I cry as I write this, and my tears strike the page like raindrops. My death was arranged some time ago. I imported the person to take care of it in the fastest and least painful manner I could imagine — it is the means by which I died as Carmen, in my most successful movie 'Programmed to Kill.' In that movie, I am standing on a bed, and I am shot from the ground. It had the passion of a great death, so I will recreate this, only this time, it is not Carmen, it is me, and it is for real. For obvious reasons, I cannot disclose my assassin because he is doing me a great mercy, and he must not be charged — he is my Archangel Michael. This knowledge I implore you to keep secret. There will be an insurance claim, the proceeds of which will benefit the lives of my brother and sister. If the insurer discovers the means of my death, the policy will be cancelled. I am sorry to burden you with this responsibility, my darling, but you are the only person I can really trust. My diaries are for your eyes only.

"I fear not death, my love, but I do fear leaving you. Please look after my sister Beleza, and please love her as you love me. I make my final exit from this grand stage, proud that I have achieved much in life ... I have loved and been loved ... I leave behind a small legacy of films, but above all else, I leave you a memory of us that will remain forever in your heart. In my will, I asked to be buried with these words etched on my tombstone: 'I would never have achieved the things I have in love and in life had it not been for my hubris.'

"I love you, Axis Stone — remember me always. Malika."

Misting up, I glanced back at her portrait and took a gulp of coffee.

CHAPTER TWENTY-ONE

I T WAS BLATANTLY obvious that Maurice, the gardener, had been hired to do the dastardly deed. I put the mug on the desk, reached into my hip pocket, took out the opal, and slipped it into the secret chamber together with the diaries. Then, I closed and locked the compartment. I would abide by Malika's wishes and keep her diaries secret.

The diaries had given me reason to rethink everything. My coffee was cold, so I went back to the poolside for a refill from the jug. Along the way, I emptied the remaining contents of the mug into a pot plant that looked like it needed it. Then I poured a fresh brew from the jug and slumped into a deckchair. The hot coffee tasted good and helped me think. I figured my initial guess must have been right: Maurice must have done the job according to Malika's wishes and then left her on the bed in a dramatic, albeit blood-drenched, pose. The question I found difficult to reconcile was why, if she loved me, would she leave herself in such a gross state for me to find? Surely, she could have taken pills or something infinitely less gory. Then the thought struck me that she might have planned for Dorris to find her and not me. The realisation caused me to yell out the name "Dorris!" I'd forgotten there was a person other than Santana, Mansfield, Murphy, and Beleza who knew I was staying at the house: Dorris! She could easily be the weak link. I jumped up and paced up and down the length of the pool, mulling it over in my head.

What if instead of Dorris discovering the body as intended, Volt had? So where was Dorris when I got to the house? Maybe Dorris didn't find her at all. Then it struck me: where did Dorris come from in the first place? I rushed back to the den, opened the secret panel again, got the diaries out, and manically thumbed through them in search of the first mention of Dorris, and found it. Malika had hired Dorris only eight months ago. She had come recommended by none other than Lexi Diamond! That instantly made Dorris a serious security risk and led to another thought: how did Malika find Maurice? I speed-read on and came up with the answer: Dorris had recommended Maurice for the job! Now I was on edge. What if Dorris had leaked to Lexi about the planned assisted suicide: the how, when, and why of it? What if, as a result, Volt knew, then he conveniently turned up to take credit for the murder, knowing that sooner or later the cops would discover the truth and then let him off the hook? Is that why he hasn't blown town? I sat down and finished my coffee, wondering if I was overthinking it. No ... It was a conspiracy for sure, and if I was right, Volt would be coming here today for the opal. Dorris could easily have overheard me telling Bella earlier that I'd be home all day. She could also have been out of sight, listening to my conversation with Mansfield last night, and then reported what she'd overheard to Lexi. Maybe the sick relative in the hospital had been a ruse to make an escape. The realisation struck me that Dorris hadn't feared losing her job with her employer deceased. Was that because she already had a new position with Lexi as payback for being a plant? If I told Santana, he'd have proof of the assisted suicide, and the insurance claim would be dead in the water. A conundrum ... what the hell should I do? It was obvious: arm myself. I scurried to the guest room, put on my jacket, sat on the edge of the bed, retrieved the 9 mm from under the pillow, and shoved it down the back of my jeans. Then suddenly, the room moved all on its own ... I thought, was that an earthquake? Then my head began to swim. I wasn't thinking straight — my vision had gone fuzzy. Time had momentarily been suspended — the room slowly cartwheeled, and the last thing I could think of was the coffee ... drugged, and then I slid off the bed onto the floor, out like a light.

A slap across the chops brought me round. It wasn't a gentle slap by any means and was followed by three more. My vision cleared enough to make out that the man behind the sweeping arm was Anderson Volt.

"Where the hell is it?" he growled. "Tell me or I'll knock your teeth out."

I believed him; they were already feeling loose from the previous barrage of blows.

"Hey, ease up, all right, all right," I groaned, groggily. There was a loud click, and the cold steel of a gun barrel pressed hard against my right temple.

"Get up!" he demanded.

I clambered to my feet and very nearly collapsed back in a heap on the floor.

"Damn, that coffee has a better punch than you," I groaned.

"Shut up and get the opal," he snarled.

"Then what? You give me two bullets in the brain like you did Kincade? The way I figure it, the opal is the only thing keeping me alive."

His pistol whipped across the side of my head, and my legs buckled from under me. Standing over me, he growled, "Next time, it won't be so pretty."

I could feel a lump growing on the side of my head and mumbled, "What makes you think that was chocolate-box?"

A baseball mitt-sized hand reached down, grabbed my shirt front, and hauled me to my feet.

"Get me what I want, or I'll take out your left knee. I won't ask again," he said, aiming the gun at the target.

I believed him ... lacking a sense of humour meant he wasn't the type to make idle threats.

"Okay, okay, keep your shirt on ... it's in another room, in a safe place."

He raised his hand to strike.

"No more whacks, for God's sake, or I won't be able to find the bloody thing."

He shoved me towards the door. I needed to think about how to draw my gun before he could get off a shot at me, but he was too close. I wouldn't stand a chance. It was obvious he was going to shoot me as soon as I handed over the opal. I led him to the door of the den and stopped.

"Hands on your head," he demanded.

Now I was sunk. I had to comply.

He opened the door.

"I need to go behind the desk ... there's a locked drawer. I have the key."

"Do it, one false move and you're dead."

I used the light switch by the door to turn on the light, then took the key out of my pocket, dangled it in front of him, and went around behind the desk. He kept the gun trained on me. I took out the top drawer and then opened the secret compartment, reached in, withdrew the opal, locked it back up, and then slid the drawer back into place.

"Give it to me!" he ordered.

"You have to be careful not to drop it. Opals are very delicate."

I leaned across the desk and placed the opal in his open palm. As soon as his fingers closed around it, I clapped my hands hard and dived for the letter opener on the desk. The lights went out—the room plunged into darkness—there was a bright muzzle flash from his gun—I lunged at him with the letter opener. The bullet missed me, but I didn't miss him—the letter opener found his thigh, and he let out a howl. I reached for my gun, but he was already out the door. Fighting off the light-headedness from the dope, I very nearly toppled over trying to grope my way through the darkness past the desk. When I reached the hallway, I saw him limping out through the front door, leaving a trail of blood dotting the floor in his wake.

I took aim with the gun in both hands and yelled, "Stop or you're dead, Volt!"

There was no way I'd be able to hit him with my aim wobbling about like a drunk trying to walk a white line. I squeezed off a round just as he slipped outside, and the bullet took a chunk out of the door. Chasing as fast as my wobbly legs could carry me, I made for the front door and then stopped outside. Scanning the scene along the barrel of my pistol, there was no sign of him, only dots of blood on the driveway leading to the street. I followed them, then heard an engine start up, tyres squeal, and a car roar off. Standing kerbside, sucking in big breaths, I was thankful it didn't come to a shootout. He might have got away with the opal, but at least I'd got away with my life.

My suspicion that Dorris had been the informant was now vindicated: she'd drugged my coffee. I expected never to hear from her again.

~ ~ ~

I went back inside, and on the dining room table, I found the passport I'd given Sonny Rivers as security. Volt had left it there. Al Head and company had no idea I'd replaced it with a new one. It was a clear message from Head to leave town. I poured myself a JD and skulled it, topped it up, went out onto the patio, and sank into a deckchair. The coffee pot was still on the table, reminding me of the clever way I'd been duped. It was an alarming wake-up call to the cunning of my adversary. Nearly lunchtime, I figured there was nothing to be gained from sitting on my butt. Volt had made his house call, got what he wanted, and was unlikely to make a second appearance, so I decided to take a ride in the fresh air down to Sunset. As it turned out, I just kept on riding to Hollywood Boulevard. It was time for a reprieve from all the crap I'd been dealing with—time to chill and take in a few tourist sights—the Walk of Fame, The Chinese Theatre.

I arrived back at the house just before 3 p.m. and found Bella sunning herself by the pool. She'd figured from the blood spots on the floor something bad had happened. I filled her in on the confrontation with Volt and told her why Dorris wouldn't be coming back. She was shocked. Her meeting with the insurance company hadn't gone according to plan. They had a preliminary police report that suspected voluntary assisted suicide. The claim had been put on hold until the coroner's report.

"You might need to prepare for the report not being in your favour," I told her compassionately.

"I know. But my sister was insured, so I must go through with ze claim... it was vat she wanted."

I picked up the coffee pot still on the table.

"This very nearly got me killed ... enough to turn a guy off coffee forever."

"You haven't said hello to me yet, darling," she purred through a warm smile.

"I'm sorry," I said, putting down the jug. "I guess the morning got the better of me."

I leaned down and kissed her soft lips. We made love, and it was blissful. They say beautiful women don't always make the best lovers because they think they've got enough going for them with their looks. Well, this beauty, just like her sister, was the total exception to that claim. She made love with the passion of a tigress.

When spent, with our hearts pounding, we clung breathlessly to one another, as though we were the last couple on the planet. To me, she was heaven on earth—lost in the fervor of such passionate lovemaking, for me, the heady experience was incredibly rare.

CHAPTER TWENTY-TWO

'THE TERRIBLE TANGO' broke the rapture of the moment. I fumbled around in the pile of clothes on the floor for my phone, found it, and answered.

"Axis Stone ... hey Nick, you've landed. You found Dan? excellent."

"Yeah, I'll text you the address. Okay, see you in an hour or so."

Bella smiled gracefully, "I'll freshen up and change for your guests, darling."

I slipped into the pool for a couple of laps.

~ ~ ~

An hour later, we were both dressed in our best casual threads, sitting in the lounge room with a JD in hand, expecting the doorbell to ring at any moment.

"Do you think you will be able to get ze opal back?" she said softly.

"I'm not counting on it," I admitted.

"What will ze owner think?" she asked.

"I'll cross that bridge when I come to it."

"Maybe zere will be something of value at ze ranch?"

"Possibility. I have to admit I'm still not sold on you coming along, risking your life, especially now we've—"

She cut me off, putting her finger on my lips. "Shush, darling, zere will be no negotiation. Zis is my life to risk. Do you worry I might be an imposition?"

"No, no, you said you can handle a gun, and if you're anything like your sister, you have the bravado ... I just don't want to see you hurt after losing…"

"I know vat you are saying, darling. You will just have to get used to thinking of me as a member of ze team, okay?"

We heard a car pull up in the driveway. I gave her a peck on the lips and then said, "Must be them, I'll get the door."

I opened the front door to Nick and Dan and gave Nick a big welcoming hug. Dan, in his customary ice-cold manner, managed a handshake and something of an excuse for a smile. Dan looked like the Filipino version of Charles Bronson, scars and all.

They were travelling light, only a small kitbag each. I led them inside and introduced them to Beleza, who then showed them their respective rooms.

They dumped their bags and then Beleza brought them back for a drink. Of course, being a teetotaller, Dan settled for an orange juice.

"How's your health, Dan?" I asked because he'd been wounded in the line of duty in the case I had in Manila a while back.

"No problema, Mr Stone," he growled. His grin showing off two gold front teeth.

"Love the new teeth, my friend."

"Axis, I need to call my friend to arrange the chopper," Nick said, as debonair as ever, commanding attention. "He can have a pilot deliver it to a heliport nearby. The closest is in West Hollywood, but it's private."

"Can we contact the owner of the heliport?" I asked.

"That would be the Sheriff, it's on the rooftop of the Santa Monica Police Station," he said with an ironic chuckle.

"Okay, I might be able to arrange that. I'll call Detective Santana soon and get him over for a meeting once we're finished. He should be able to sort out clearance."

"I have listed what we will need," Dan said gruffly, handing me an iPad. At six-feet, Dan was tall by Filipino standards, and at forty years of age, the battle scars on his face bore testament to the numerous military campaigns he'd survived as a commando. His take-no-prisoner attitude, three-pack-a-day gravel voice, and his loyalty to Nick spoke volumes about the big feller. He was physically cut like a bodybuilder, with a clean-shaven head and a big square jaw that made him scary. On the other hand, you wouldn't pick Nick as being a Filipino or a warrior. Aristocratic, educated, sophisticated, and handsome, he carried no scars on the outside. In his early forties and the monarch of one of the wealthiest families in the Philippines, Nick is the epitome of the Asian playboy hunk, as well as being one hell of a good guy. Though we made an odd trio, it sure worked for us in the Manila kidnapping case. Had he not been injured during it, Dan would've accompanied Nick and myself in the next one we'd solved: the shark arm case.

I read the notes on Dan's iPad. "That's a helluva lot of firepower, man, are you sure we'll need it all?"

"Better to be safe than sorry," Dan said sternly.

"Dan and I talked it over, we don't know what we're getting into, the ranch could be fortified, that's not uncommon with US gun laws as they are," Nick maintained.

"Yeah, I suppose you're right, I keep forgetting we're not in Australia. If you landed a chopper unannounced on a ranch in the outback there, you'd most likely be greeted with an ice-cold beer— not a gun."

That got a laugh.

Bella was standing behind me, reading the list over my shoulder.

"I would prefer a Heckler & Koch MP5 over the Uzi, Dan, but zat is my personal taste, of course," she commented and raised eyebrows.

"I wasn't sure if we could get MP5s. But if we can, then I agree with you," Dan said.

It was a win for Bella. I wasn't sure what Dan and Nick would think of her coming along, but from their reaction, my reservations seemed to be unwarranted.

"The second page is my strategy. It's open for discussion," Dan said.

Nick hadn't seen it, so we crowded around the iPad to study.

"So, you think two vehicles on the ground and the chopper in a simultaneous raid?" I submitted.

"Yes, the chopper to land inside the perimeter fence and the vehicles to go through them. That will cover the sound of the early warning signal from the approaching chopper and also provide a delay just after landing, a critical moment," Dan explained.

Nick asked, "How many personnel?"

"I said, "Two in each car and three in the chopper, so seven."

"We need four more?" Dan said.

"Only three, Dan, zere are four of us," Bella corrected him.

Nick's expression seemed to question Bella for a moment, but then he put it aside.

Nick queried, "When are you thinking of going in?"

"Day or night, Dan?" I added.

"I'm thinking in twenty-two hours at 0300," Dan said firmly.

"Okay, it's 1700 hours now, we'll see if Detective Santana concurs," I said.

"Fine," Dan agreed.

I had the basis of a plan to discuss with Santana. Dan showed us military satellite images of the ranch. He'd mapped the required route by land and air, factoring in the chopper and vehicles arriving at the ranch simultaneously. Then he'd used a floor plan of the ranch to formulate the ground assault.

I phoned Santana and asked him to join us.

~ ~ ~

By the time I'd freshened up the drinks, the doorbell rang.

"I'll get it," I said, heading towards the door.

I let Santana in. "Carlos, just before we join the others, I had a brush with our friend Volt today."

"I'm not surprised ... it was only a matter of time. I'm amazed you're still standing. When was this?"

"This morning."

"And you're only telling me now?" he growled, noticeably pissed off.

"I needed to know a few things first."

He grated his teeth and growled angrily, "We're talking about a wanted murderer here!"

He was a different bloke when he got angry, fearsome. I tried to placate his temper and quieten him down. "I know, I know, keep your shirt on ... just hear me out."

"Hear you out? Christ, that's all I seem to be doing ... it's you that's not doing the listening."

"Mate, the policing of my thoughts is way out of your jurisdiction—"

Just as our heated discussion was about to boil over, Bella arrived and saved the day. I don't know whether it was female intuition or not, but she sure as hell saved my butt from an embarrassing kicking. I could tell by the look on Santana's face that I would have been on the losing end of his verbal joust.

"This lovely man must be Detective Santana," Bella said warmly. She held out her hand for him to take.

He snapped out of his mood and took it.

I made the introductions with a contrived smile. "Detective Santana, this is Malika's sister, Beleza del Mundo."

Santana cracked a tight smile and said sympathetically. "Please accept my condolences, Miss del Mundo."

"Call me Bella, and thank you, Detective."

"Let's drop the formalities. My friends call me Carlos."

He glanced at me. I realised then he was referring to me as a friend.

Bella took Carlos by the arm and walked him into the living room, where I introduced him to Nick and Dan.

"Can I get you a drink, Carlos?" Bella asked politely.

"Yeah, well, I'm officially off duty, so I guess I'll take a JD on the rocks, thank you, ma'am."

I gestured for us to sit.

"Okay, as far as we're all concerned, this is off the police record," I explained. "Dan here has come up with an assault plan on the ranch. I'll hand it over to him to walk us through."

Bella brought Carlos a drink, and he listened intently as Dan showed us the images on his iPad and talked us through the strategy. When Dan had finished, we waited for comments. To be honest, I was expecting some resistance from Carlos, so it came as a surprise when there was none.

"I can arrange for the chopper to land at Santa Monica, but we won't be able to load arms there. I suggest we do that in a more discrete location than under the nose of the police department. As for weapons, I can provide everything on your list, but I'd prefer MP5s over Uzis," Santana said.

Bella fired us all a big I-told-you-so smirk.

Nick asked Santana, "Where do we assemble then?"

"I think we should drive to Vegas, pick up the chopper there, and rendezvous with my two colleagues. They'll provide weapons and assault vehicles," Santana explained.

I queried, "How long from here to Vegas?"

"A four-hour drive, give or take," Santana said.

Dan spoke up. "Who are your colleagues?"

"Former Vegas cops, good men, also with a score to settle with Head."

"And you, are you coming?" Dan added.

"It's the only way I can keep it all under the police radar," Santana said grimly. "Besides, who'd wanna miss out on a good old-fashioned shootout," he joked.

That lightened things up, and we all had a chuckle.

Nick summarised the discussion. "Well, all I need is the location for the chopper in Vegas, then I can lock down the arrangements."

"I've already checked that out," Santana said matter-of-factly. "We've got permission to use the heliport atop the Western Pacific Trust Building in downtown Vegas. Just need to get them the flight plan, ETA, etcetera."

"What happens with the flight plan of the chopper after the assault?" I wondered out loud. "Won't it leave a suspicious footprint?"

Dan had the answer. "No, I have an exit strategy. I'll fly you and Nick in the chopper to Frisco, to hook up with a flight to Sydney."

Carlos shot Dan a questioning glare. "You a licensed pilot as well?"

Dan replied with a self-assured nod.

"So, four of us in two vehicles and three in the chopper," Dan confirmed.

"Does that work for you, Carlos?" I asked.

"Four? I only count three," Carlos said with a furrowed brow.

"I am coming too," Bella told Carlos with a resolute expression.

There came a pregnant pause while Carlos mentally mulled the idea over. You could see the wheels turning in his mind, and then he arrived at a decision. "Okay," he replied without question. "My guys have the local knowledge to implement the plan."

"Good, zen it is settled," Bella said. "Time to eat, I will order in food. Does everybody like Japanese?"

Nick called his friend with the chopper and concluded the arrangements. With it done, Santana called his security contact at the Western Pacific Trust Building for landing clearance.

After dinner, Santana and I sat alone by the pool for a private chat.

"We didn't finish our discussion about Volt," Santana said caustically.

"Have your say, Carlos. I've got no cause to argue with you," I said.

"You put yourself in a compromising situation, Axis. You could have gotten yourself killed, and that would have put me right in the shit. Do you understand that? You've got no choice but to work with me here, son, or none of this will happen. I've worked hard for my gold watch, and I don't plan to be wearing it pushing up daisies," Santana replied.

"I hear you," I acknowledged.

I explained what happened in greater detail. Santana acquiesced once I mentioned the diaries, the passport, Dorris drugging me, and Bella arriving while I was recovering ... I stretched the truth a little, not prepared to take the responsibility of killing the insurance claim. The proof that Volt hadn't killed Malika had also changed Santana's official involvement.

"No excuses, but I didn't know what to do after giving up the opal, I just needed to clear my head," I admitted.

"It still doesn't let Volt off the hook. I've got him pencilled in for murder one of Kincade and Kovacs," Santana stated.

"At least I stabbed him in the leg with a letter opener, so he'd have to be hobbling around with a bloody sore thigh ... that should slow him down some," I remarked.

"Good, I'll put Murphy onto checking doctors and hospitals. We'll get him. It's a damn shame the girl and her brother will lose the insurance money, and you've lost the opal," Santana said.

That wasn't what Bella would want to hear. "I think a good lawyer will get them some sort of settlement from the insurance company," I said hopefully. "They've got Gerry Mansfield, he's a hot shot. I'll just have to worry about the opal later."

"Good call ... I should get Murphy to bring in Dorris," Santana said, reaching for his phone.

"No, no, not yet ... not until we're done. We need to keep the leaks plugged until then," I said sternly. "Besides, we might need to use her. One thing bothers me ... are you sure you're okay with coming along, mate? There'll probably be bullets flying around everywhere and—"

"Don't worry about me, pale-face. I only got to being this long in the tooth by dodging bullets," Santana reassured me, reaching into his inside pocket and producing a flash drive. "You'll want to show what's on this to the others." He handed it over. "Satellite shots of Al Head's ranch, which, by the way, is called Little Bohemia ... the shots differ somewhat from those Dan showed us. These show people and vehicle movements over the course of the last 24 hours."

Nick wandered out onto the patio carrying a bottle of JD. He held it up and announced, "Is this a private chat, or can I cut in with a refill?"

"Pour away, brother," I told Nick happily. "Carlos just said Head's ranch is called Little Bohemia."

"Wasn't that the name of John Dillinger's hideout?" Nick questioned.

"Now here's a guy who knows his American history," Carlos declared.

After we had topped our glasses, I raised mine and said, "Cheers to better days."

We toasted optimistically to what we hoped would result from our combined efforts.

CHAPTER TWENTY-THREE

D AN OPENED THE flash drive on his laptop and checked the images.

"This is excellent recon. I can see seven vehicles in and out ... and can count, one, two ... six perimeter guards with dogs on leads," Dan remarked.

"Yeah, they each have a set routine, see here..." Santana pointed at the screen. "This dude with the guard dog makes his round from the rear of the house, goes to the barn, then to a gate and then back again — takes him all of fifteen minutes — once every two hours. By the way, you didn't get this from me," Carlos said, with a wry smile and a raised eyebrow.

"With all that security, they must be hiding something of value," Dan observed.

Armed with the satellite images, Dan was set to burn the midnight oil reworking his attack strategy.

"I want you guys out of the States within twelve hours of the assault," Santana said sternly.

I had the answer. "We're gonna pick up a flight to Sydney from Frisco."

Dan looked up from the iPad and nodded. "It's factored in."

Bella let Dan use the den to re-draft his plan.

I saw Santana out to his car. He climbed in, and I held the door open.

He eyeballed me. "I like your friends. You sure about the girl coming along?"

"I have a sneaking suspicion she can cut it. I think she's worth the risk — can't deny she's got a score to settle," I replied.

Santana started his car. "Okay, I hear ya."

I ambled back into the living room to join Nick and Bella, who were in deep conversation. Nick was busy telling her the story of meeting Rod in Winton, which, of course, led to me getting the case.

"Yeah, I don't quite know what to tell the guys back home now I've lost the opal," I admitted shamefully.

"I don't think you can be blamed for zat, honey," Bella said warmly.

"No, that's not their speed. Anyhow, something will save the day, you mark my words ... It seems to always happen that way for you, doesn't it, Axis?" Nick said with a droll smile.

I raised my glass and toasted. "Here's luck for you guys crossing the Pacific Ocean to the Americas to help save the day!"

"I'll drink to zat," Bella agreed cheerfully.

It felt good having Nick and Dan on board. Inwardly, I hoped that having Bella, Carlos, and his two colleagues with us would prove to be the right move.

Bella checked the time, and it was close to midnight. She bid us both goodnight and headed for her bedroom.

Nick said covertly watching her leave, "Don't tell me you've been there?"

I replied with a look that could only be taken one way.

"I can't believe you. What about her sister?"

I repeated the look.

"No, you're kidding me? And Lexi Diamond?"

Again, I was forced to repeat the same look but this time with a scrunched-up nose, like yes, unfortunately.

"Axis, you're despicable," he said, shocked.

"What am I supposed to do when women throw themselves at me?"

"Resist, Axis, resist."

"Why?"

"Yeah well, I suppose you're right. I'm just jealous, I guess. How pretty was the sister?"

"Come on, Daffy Duck, I'll show you something."

I led him to the den.

~ ~ ~

We found Dan busy behind the desk, toiling away so assiduously he didn't even notice us enter. I showed Nick the portrait of Malika on the wall.

"Uncanny," he cawed, "she's as beautiful as Bella, and look at all the movies she starred in ... and the photos. There she is with Jack Nicholson and here with Marion Cotillard. Boy oh boy, didn't she travel in some exclusive company."

I led Nick back to the living room so as not to disturb Dan any further.

We topped up our drinks, and I told him the sad story of what had happened to poor Malika. He was most interested when I admitted that I had fallen in love with her.

"Axis, I've never heard you mention the four-letter L-word before."

"I've never heard myself mention it either, but you know it feels like I lost Malika and gained Bella, and that it was somehow destined to be."

"Poor girl, it must have been devastating to realise the dream was over at such a young age."

"And what about the way she chose to end it?" I said dispiritedly.

"I can see it has affected you, mate. Do you think if we get through this, you might settle down with Bella?"

"No. I think she might follow in her sister's footsteps, and I wouldn't want to get in the way of that."

Nick looked surprised. "That's very noble of you, Kemosabe."

"Yeah, I know, weird isn't it? I must be getting old."

Once we had drained the last remaining drop from the bottle of JD, we decided to hit the sack. We both knew tomorrow promised to be a massive day.

I was on my way to my room, thinking grimly to myself that if things were to go wrong tomorrow, it might well be my last day on the planet, when I noticed a light shining under the door of the main bedroom. The dreadful thoughts made me want to bid goodnight to Bella, and you never know, I might just get lucky, so I tapped gently on the door with my knuckle. After a minute or two and no answer, just as I was about to head off to bed, the door creaked open enough for a hand to emerge and an index finger to beckon me inside. The morbid thoughts instantly evaporated when I slipped into the bedroom and found Bella in bed.

When I woke up next to her in the morning, I gently kissed her awake.

She stared at me with those beautiful blue eyes and still sleepy mumbled sadly, "Zat might be ze last time we ever make love."

Her eyes were misting up. "Let's not go there," I said warmly. "I'd like to think we're both bulletproof." I pecked her lips and smiled playfully.

That cheered her up. It was normal that as the day progressed, as experienced as we might be, each of us would still end up with a knot in our stomachs — going into battle has an effect you never quite get used to.

I walked out onto the patio to join Nick and Dan. The stunning Californian dawn greeted us — the air smelled fresh, and the rising sun was warm on my face. Though I hadn't slept much, it felt good to be alive.

"G'day, guys ... What time did you finish up, Dan?" I asked.

"Oh, I don't know, but I got a bit of sleep," he replied wearily.

"The satellite shots showed there were CCTV cameras around the ranch perimeter fence that we hadn't noticed ... and one on the road leading to the ranch," Nick explained. "Isn't that right, Dan?"

"Yeah, it means we'll need to knock it out first, or we'll lose the element of surprise," Dan confirmed.

Bella joined us, looking fresh as a daisy and as stunning as ever.

"Good morning, gentlemen. I see you've made coffee. Zere will be a delivery of fresh croissants for us in a few minutes. I'll get ze condiments ready," she said cheerfully.

"You think of everything, baby," I said affectionately.

'The Terrible Tango' sounded on my phone. I took the call. "Carlos, g'day. Okay ... so we'll pick you up there at noon — fine — no, we'll find it. Yes, an SUV. Dan studied them and found CCTV cameras, oh, you too? Yeah, we'll have plenty of travel time to talk about it on the road. Alright, see you then." I put the phone away and lowered myself into a deckchair. Then I told everyone, "Carlos is texting me an address in Marina Del Rey to collect him at noon. We'll leave for Vegas from there."

"Have we got a vehicle?" Nick asked.

"We'll take the SUV in the garage so that Bella and Carlos can use it to return from Vegas afterward," I said. "Carlos found the CCTV as well, said it kept him up half the night thinking if there were more, and then he found the one on the side of the road. He said we'll need to knock it out first, like you said, Dan."

"Great minds," Dan chuckled.

Bella arrived with a tray of fresh croissants, strawberry jam, and honey — we dug in.

~ ~ ~

Later, I packed my port, following Santana's advice to quickly leave the United States after the assault to avoid repercussions. Bella, with her US citizenship, would stay at Malika's house under the watchful eye of Santana and Gerry Mansfield. As for Nick, Dan, and myself, we would catch the first available flight from San Francisco to Sydney.

I strapped on my shoulder holster snugly under my leather jacket, finding comfort in the extra sense of security it provided. We gathered in the garage and boarded the SUV.

"Classy car, these things cost a packet," Dan observed.

Nick took the driver's seat, being more accustomed to driving on that side of the road than me. I glanced longingly at the Harley parked in front of the Beamer.

"I'm going to miss that bike," I moaned.

Bella spoke up from the back seat next to Dan, "It will be waiting here for your return. After all, it is yours. Or do you want me to ship it to Australia?"

"No, I'd rather make it another excuse for coming back here once the heat is off."

"I'm glad you said zat, darling," she purred.

She was dressed in a fancy black jumpsuit, resembling a Formula One driver's outfit.

"You're dressed for the job, ma'am," Dan observed.

"Designer attack gear. I wear it ven free falling. I thought it was so nicely camouflaged, it would be good for ze nighttime sortie," she explained sincerely.

That opened up a conversation topic for the adventurous duo. They chatted about their experiences with rock climbing, white water rafting, bungee jumping, paragliding — you name it, if it could kill you, they were into it. They were still enthusiastically sharing their stories when we arrived at the rendezvous with Santana in Marina Del Rey. I was shocked to discover that the address led us to a moored boat. Nick seemed right in his element, but just the sight of it made me feel seasick. Reluctant to walk out onto the floating jetty, I sent Nick to fetch Santana.

"Why aren't you going, Axis?" Bella asked with a smirk.

"Because I'm allergic to boats, that's why," I snapped.

"He discovered that in the Philippines," Dan chimed in wryly.

"Oh, poor baby," Bella sympathetically said, rubbing my short-cropped hair as if I were her pet dog.

Within minutes, Nick and Carlos appeared on the wharf, each carrying a kit bag that seemed heavy with weapons. As we watched, two blondes in string bikinis and high heels walked past our car, headed for a boat moored in the marina. They certainly brightened my day, and I couldn't help but think that this place, with its luxurious boats and beautiful women, would be the ideal location for a bachelor pad. If only I had the time.

"Zere are plenty of distractions here for you, Axis, huh?" Bella reminded me over my shoulder. I realised she had me figured out, but I wasn't sure if it was to my advantage or not.

With the kit bags safely stored in the trunk, we hit the road to Vegas.

CHAPTER TWENTY-FOUR

"**YOU LOOK DIFFERENT** today, Carlos," Bella said conversationally.

"Other folks have said that too, reckon I must go through some sort of metamorphosis when I take time off being a cop," Carlos replied.

"Similar thing happens to me as soon as I board my boat," Nick added from behind the wheel.

"Yeah well, if I was getting off a boat I'd sure look different, green-faced from throwing up," I chuckled.

Carlos asked, "Sailing doesn't agree with you, Axis?"

"He says he's allergic to it, don't you darling?" Bella smirked.

"I'm a one hundred percent landlubber," I admitted, carefully changing the subject. Talking about boats was making me queasy. "Everything set with your colleagues, Carlos?"

"It's all apple-pie, they're waiting for us to arrive," he rasped.

Nick asked, "What will you do with the prisoners?"

"Good question. I'll take 'em back into California to be charged. I've arranged for Lieutenant Murphy to be on standby for that," Carlos explained.

"How will you explain your involvement?" I queried.

"Undercover duty, of course," Carlos answered with a sardonic smirk. "I asked for volunteers for the job yesterday."

"Who did you ask?" I quizzed.

"Why me, of course ... and I accepted," Carlos replied.

That got a laugh from us, but we also knew he was being shrewd.

"You sure you'll be able to handle those three all the way back to L.A.?" I asked.

"So," Carlos said more seriously. "There will be three vehicles, this one and the two of my colleagues. We'll put a prisoner in each, hand and foot cuffed, drive them to Baker, a small town just over the border in California, only thirty minutes from the ranch. There, they'll be charged under my jurisdiction and jailed. Really, I don't expect to take Head prisoner, do you?"

"To be honest, no. I only expect Lexi to give up," I said.

"Yeah, well, if it's only her, then it won't be a problem. We'll just take her back with us. I'll charge her with conspiracy to murder," Carlos explained.

"Vat sort of sentence would zat be?" Bella asked.

"Probably life, but she'd get out within ten for a first offence," Carlos replied.

"Gosh, zat's a fair chunk out of someone's life," Bella exclaimed.

Carlos posed poetically, "Don't do the crime if you can't do the time, miss."

"Just weapons in the kit bags, Carlos?" I asked.

"I was wondering when you'd get around to that. No, there's an operating Stingray in one of them," Carlos revealed.

"A Stingray? What's that?" I asked curiously.

"Oh, a fancy piece of gadgetry," he mumbled.

"We've got four hours of driving ahead of us, and I promise I won't shut up about it until you tell me what it is," Nick declared from behind the wheel.

"A cell-site simulator," Carlos finally explained. "It operates by mimicking the towers of major telecom companies. When someone's phone connects to the spoofed network, it transmits a unique identification code, and through the characteristics of its radio signals when they reach the receiver, information is learned about the phone's location. It's operating now, monitoring all four of Al Head's cell numbers. Two for Sonny Rivers, one for Lexi Diamond, and one for Anderson Volt."

"How the heck did you get those numbers?" I asked.

"Oh, I played the terrorism and drug trafficking card yesterday in relation to Mr Head, and that got me the Stingray. It only works in a 400-mile radius, but that gives me plenty of warning. My colleagues Max and Will are bringing along a Cyberhawk drone ... now that's one hell of a piece of cool technology," Carlos explained.

"Love it," Nick erupted. "We used a cellphone jamming device on the kidnapping case in Manila, and it worked a treat, didn't it, Axis?"

"Nick loves technology," I pointed out.

"Nick, why don't I drive?" Santana suggested. "I know the road, and if I speed, I can't get busted."

Nick was happy to hand over the wheel, and he snuggled in beside Bella on the back seat with Dan, who was asleep. Santana took over driving, and soon enough, the rest of us were snoring away.

~ ~ ~

Interstate 15 took us right into Las Vegas. Santana woke us up on the late final approach to the city, just past 4 p.m.

"Rise and shine, kiddies. We've hit the golden mile," he announced musically.

He wasn't wrong. Even in daylight, the place was lit up like a circus. Santana turned into South Las Vegas Boulevard and wheeled into the car park of Dougie Js Café.

We were happy to get out of the car and stretch our legs. It was the legal section of town, with the US General Services Administration Building opposite and a couple of banks on the intersection of East Bonneville Avenue.

"The Western Pacific Trust building is just up the street. Will and Max will meet us at the café at five," Carlos said, holding the arch of his back and wincing in pain.

"The drive tough on your back?" I asked.

"Yeah, I'll be okay after a stretch," Carlos replied.

"There's an ATM across the road. I need to get some cash," I said. Carlos nodded. "Okay, we'll meet you in the café."

"Guys?" I said to the others, "I'm going to the ATM across the road. See you in the café."

I dodged the light traffic, crossed over East Bonneville Avenue, and used the ATM. On the way back, the traffic had jammed at the traffic lights, forcing me to slip between cars. As I was passing in front of a car, the traffic began to move, and a car stopped abruptly for me. I looked through the windscreen at the driver to wave a thank you and nearly dropped dead—it was Lexi, and she was staring at me with her mouth dropped open, as if I'd been resurrected from the dead. I went to the driver's side of the car, and she wound the window down.

"It is you! What on Earth are you doing in Vegas?" she gasped in shock.

She was holding up the traffic, and the cars behind had begun honking. I had to shout to get over the ruckus. "Get a park and meet me in Dougie Js Café there on the corner ... we need to talk."

The honking was getting over the top. I threw my hands in the air at the line of cars behind her and scowled at them. There really wasn't much point; they were in the right.

"Okay, see you there," Lexi bellowed, and then drove off.

I finished crossing the road and stood kerbside, wondering if I'd done the right thing, cursing myself that I'd probably given her time to let Al Head know I was in town.

I rushed into the café and found the others sitting in a cubicle by a window.

"What's up?" Santana asked. "You look like you've seen a ghost!"

I whipped off my sunglasses and pinched the bridge of my nose, my head aching. "I can't believe it. Of all the rotten luck, crossing the bloody road, a car stopped for me, and behind the wheel was the last person you'd expect to see: Lexi Diamond. And she was looking right at me! I even waved to her for stopping before the penny dropped!"

"Damn! So, did she recognise you?" Santana said with a groan.

The others had astonished looks on their faces.

"You bet she did. I spoke to her ... had no alternative but to invite her to the café for a coffee and a chat."

"You should've jumped into the car with her. She'll probably phone Head," Santana said, a dour expression on his craggy face.

"I know, I know, but what's done is done ... look, she only knows Santana and me, so I'll get a table on my own. Carlos, you sit with these guys, your back to Lexi so she won't recognise you."

"Okay, I'll book you a room at Cabana Suites, it's just nearby ... do you think you can get her back there?" Santana questioned.

"I guess I can try," I said shamelessly.

Nick gave me a wry smile.

Bella raised an eyebrow.

"You get her out of here. I'll follow you and then bust her in the room. We'll have to keep her there. Bella, you'll have to guard her overnight," Santana submitted.

Bella didn't want to miss out on the ranch assault. "Why me? I'm no babysitter," she snarled angrily.

I said hastily, "We'll discuss it later. She'll be here any minute."

"As should Will and Max," Santana added.

"Damn, it never rains, it pours," I complained.

I went across the room, found a cubicle by a window, and was just about to sit down when I saw her walk past the window outside to enter. I sat, leaving the seat opposite so she'd have her back to the others. When she found me, I stood gentlemanly to greet her. She removed her sunglasses and offered me a curt smile.

In a sexy knee-length striped summery dress that clung to her body like cling-wrap, leaving little for the imagination, her long tanned legs, lovely sandaled feet, and blonde hair tied up, she looked very much at home in Vegas. I gave her a peck on the cheek, and then we both sat.

"Don't you look good enough to eat," I said flirtatiously.

"I'm still getting over seeing you, of all people ... they say only six degrees separates all of us, well, this sure beats that, I think," she said with a confused expression, mostly reserved for blonde jokes. I kind of got what she was trying to say.

"I decided to visit the gambling capital of the world before leaving for Sydney. So, here I am," I lied expertly.

"Oh, I see. So how long are you in town?"

"Only a day or two, then I'll fly out. Did you hear about Malika?"

"Yes, I was told it was suicide. I couldn't believe it..."

She looked tearful, but it wasn't worthy of a cigar, average acting.

"Voluntary assisted suicide, the cops reckon. It must have been such a shock for you," I said facetiously.

"Dorris rang me crying ... I ... I didn't know what to say."

Pair of conspirators, I thought. "Yeah, I bet you didn't," I mumbled.

"I had no idea she was as sick as that," she lied.

"Yes, seems it came as a surprise for all of us."

I took her hand and peered into her eyes. "I suppose you're still in mourning?" I slipped the other hand under the table and fondled her bare knee. She didn't flinch.

"I feel guilty not being there for her, Axis. But you know, with everything to do with Carson, I ... I just needed some space," she said, displaying some excitement at my touch. "Where are you staying?" she groaned, her voice faltering.

"Just up the street at the Cabana Suites. I haven't checked in yet ... I only just got here. How about we go for a walk there? Do you have time?"

Her eyes rolled, and she stammered, "Um, ah, yes, I suppose so."

I withdrew my hand, stood up, nodded slyly to Santana out of Lexi's view, and flashed him three times with five fingers — fifteen minutes. Then I left.

"We can go to my car," she said on the way out of the café.

"No, it's nearly five. There'd be too many people around," I said.

She was trying to avoid going to my hotel room.

~ ~ ~

Thankfully, the check-in process at the Cabana Suites was quick. I left a message for Santana, took the keycard, and headed for the room. Once we were alone in the elevator, we kissed and groped. She was clearly excited by the time we reached the room.

Kissing fervently at the door, I managed to open it, and we nearly stumbled inside. In my imagination, I could see Santana stepping out of the elevator.

Panting and eager, Lexi pulled away and said, "I need to use the bathroom, honey." She rushed to the bathroom while I waited for Santana. Seconds later, the door opened. I gestured with my finger to my lips and then pointed towards the bathroom. Santana understood the message and drew his pistol. I sat on the bed, and we waited for her.

The toilet flushed, and then the door opened. As soon as she saw Santana, she realised it was a setup and shot me a menacing look.

"You asshole, Axis!" she growled angrily, heading towards the door.

Santana stopped her in her tracks with a strong arm. "You're not going anywhere, young lady," he snarled, and in a New York second, he had her hands cuffed behind her back.

"It seems we may have turned a negative into a positive," I said.

"Damn you both," Lexi spat, sounding like a trapped cat.

Santana checked in her pocketbook and seized her phone.

CHAPTER TWENTY-FIVE

T HE DOOR BURST open, and Bella stormed in, immediately confronting Lexi. Before Lexi could utter a word, Bella landed a solid left jab on her nose, a blow that would have made any prize-fighter envious.

"Zat's for ze way you treated my sister, you bitch!" Bella snarled, sounding like a vexed she-devil.

With her hands handcuffed, Lexi wasn't about to respond. She was knocked out cold, her expensive sculpted nose broken, with blood dripping onto the front of her dress. I grabbed a towel from the bathroom to soak up the blood.

Though Santana and I exchanged raised eyebrows we didn't say anything to Bella. We figured she had the right to hit Lexi for what she had done to Malika.

"I was a little late because I stopped to check on the stingray," Santana explained. "Our friend here called Al Head right after she saw you, so I'd say our element of surprise has been compromised."

He holstered his pistol.

"Maybe. What about Max and Will? Did they show?" I asked.

"Yeah, they're down by the pool with Nick and Dan."

I glanced at Bella. Her face was still flushed, and her eyes were fierce. She was all fired up, taking deep breaths.

Santana filled me in. "I've taken the room next to this one, just in case we need it. I suggested this place because the head of security is a buddy of mine."

"Cen get him to watch over zis bitch. If you expect me to do it, I will kill her," Bella snarled.

"Yep, I think you might just do that, kiddo," I admitted through clenched teeth.

"Okay, let me take care of that. You two go down to the pool. I'll meet you there in about fifteen minutes," Carlos suggested.

The hotel was called a retro hotel, but I think that was just an excuse for not renovating it. However, for someone like me, with a fondness for everything from the 20th century, it had a certain allure. Sure, it had seen better days, but hadn't we all? In its prime, it would have been considered a flophouse. There was a wilting, dust-laden palm tree in the lobby, and the carpet was threadbare. By the time we reached the pool, Bella had calmed down.

"You okay?" I asked as we made our way to join the others.

"Much better now. Lucky you got me out of zere. I would have scratched her eyes out. It felt good to hit her."

"I believe you, babe."

All the tables were taken. It seemed to be a popular spot, especially during happy hour. Hawaiian torches burned, setting the atmosphere while a mariachi quartet played "Guantanamera" naturally. My attention was immediately drawn to the few attractive women scattered around, most of them hanging off the arms of overweight seniors who, if they sneezed, might have toppled off their equally bloated wallets.

We took the chairs waiting for us at the two tables that had been pushed together. Nick immediately pointed towards a big, rotund guy, around forty, wearing a loose blue shirt with a white palm tree pattern all over the chest, and tan pants. His jet-black hair formed ringlets around the nape of his neck, and his deep-set, mud-coloured eyes gave him a WWF wrestler vibe. His neck was so thick that he had no chance of ever buttoning up a collar.

"Axis, this is Max Tucker," Nick announced.

The big man stood up, and the chair lifted with him as if it was glued to his butt. I extended my hand for a shake, and his baseball glove-sized mitt enveloped mine, squeezing it with a strength that made me cringe. I half-expected my knuckles to crack, and I was relieved when they didn't.

"Max, good to meet you, mate," I managed to say through clenched teeth. "That's one hell of a grip you've got there, big fella."

"I agree with you, Axis," Nick said with a snicker while flexing his digits. "I've only just regained feeling in my own fingers."

"Sorry, guys. Sometimes I just don't know my own strength," Max apologised, his distinct hillbilly accent shining through.

"And this is Will Barker," Nick added.

Will stood up. He was an unassuming-looking black guy, around forty. At first impression, he seemed ordinary, but there was something about his eyes that made the little hairs on my forearms stand at attention. Of average height, with short black curly hair and a friendly smile, a few tell-tale scars dissected both of his eyebrows, betraying his pleasant demeanour.

"Hey, Axis. Nick hasn't stopped talking about you. I must admit, I was expecting Crocodile Dundee with a slouch hat and a Bowie knife."

I shook his hand. "I change my clothes at the first sign of trouble."

"Good," he said with a chuckle. "Just like Superman, but where the hell do you find a phone booth these days?"

His quirky humour immediately endeared him to me.

"This is Beleza," I announced.

"You can call me Bella," she said with a friendly smile.

I waited for her to sit and then slid into a chair.

"Did everything go alright with Lexi?" Nick asked, sporting a derisive smirk.

"Yup, got it done. Carlos is arranging for someone to guard her. He'll be down soon." I left out the part about Bella's knockout punch.

I ordered another round of drinks, and we discussed Max and Will's connection to Carlos and Al Head. There was no love lost when Head was mentioned; both men made it clear they were eager for retribution.

Max briefed us. "Head killed our friend execution-style, with a bullet in the back of the head and one in the face to make identification difficult. Our friend Ray and his partner Lincoln were sent by the Sheriff's office to question Head about a complaint. It's a long story, but Head had been accused of ordering a hit on a high-stakes gambler who beat him in a card game. Will and I found Ray and Lincoln's bodies in a shallow grave outside-a town. Ray left behind a wife and three young children. Lincoln was just a twenty-three-year-old rookie. When the Sheriff's office dropped the investigation into the murders, both of us quit the force. I've been in the security game ever since, and Will here is a PI."

"In the same game, bro," Will said, smiling pleasantly at me.

Carlos arrived, looking a bit rattled.

"Damn! That was like pulling teeth," he grumbled, taking a chair.

"What happened, man?" I asked.

"My buddy, the head of hotel security, sent a guard to the room to watch over Lexi, but he wanted a hundred bucks an hour," he snarled.

I shook my head. "So, what happened?"

"I offered him fifty, but it took some convincing," he replied.

"Shit, he's already getting paid by the hotel, so fifty was generous," Will growled.

"Yeah, well, the guy eventually accepted the offer but insisted on giving me a list of his break times ... damn unions," Santana growled. "Anyway, let's get on with it. I'd say Al Head and his cohorts would be expecting something after Lexi called him to report seeing Axis. So, we can skip the Cyberhawk drone..."

"What were you going to do with it anyway?" Dan asked.

"Check for more cameras and booby traps on the road to the ranch," Max answered.

Dan opened his iPad on the table. "Here's the plan I've devised, taking everything we know into consideration."

Will, Max, and Carlos examined the plan while the rest of us were already familiar with it.

"So, Will and I will be in the lead car, followed by Santana and Bella, while you three launch the main assault in the chopper. Is that the gist of it?" Max asked.

Dan leaned back in his seat, folding his muscular forearms across his ripped vchest. "Yep, that's it. The critical factor is that we all arrive inside the ranch simultaneously."

"Yeah, you'll be vulnerable in the chopper just after landing, so we'll need to provide you with cover," Santana said.

"Exactly," Dan agreed.

"I was gonna use the drone to take out the camera we know is on the road," Max drawled.

Dan unfolded his arms and leaned forward, intrigued. "Reckon you can do that?"

"He sure can. He's a freaking whiz at using that thing," Will said confidently.

"But can you do it in the dark?" I asked.

"As long as I have the coordinates, I could do it in a freaking fog with my eyes shut, man," Max grinned widely.

We agreed that an hour before the planned assault, Max would use the drone to disable the camera on the road leading to the ranch.

Santana was examining Lexi's cell phone when he looked up at me.

"Lexi sent a text that said, 'I'll be at the Cabana Hotel. Meet me in the lobby at six o'clock.' It's just past that now. I don't recognise the number," he growled. "I better see who it is." He got up.

I urgently asked, "Wait! What if it's Al Head or Sonny? Won't they recognise you?"

"No, I've never met either of them, but I'd sure as hell recognise them," he snarled in reply.

"I'll keep you company," Max said, struggling to get out of his chair.

"Hey Carlos! Better turn off her phone, because it'll definitely ring when he doesn't find her in the lobby," Will warned.

Santana nodded, and they walked away.

As sundown approached, we were all growing restless. The chopper was scheduled to arrive at 2100 hours, and before that, we needed to thoroughly familiarise ourselves with the assault plan.

"When Carlos gets back, we should head up to the room to go over the plan. Maybe we should grab something to eat now. Is anyone hungry?" I asked, voicing my concerns.

"Hey, what if the person meeting Lexi gets upset that she's not there and finds out she went to your room?" Will suggested.

"Could someone do dat?" Bella questioned.

"A twenty-dollar bill will buy you that information from a bellhop in this town, lady," he replied sharply.

"You're right, Will. We better check the room," I said anxiously.

Nick cautioned, "No, Axis, it's safer for Santana to do it. Ring him."

He was right. I made the call. After a few rings, Santana answered and informed me that he didn't recognise anyone in the lobby. He agreed to check on Lexi in the room.

We waited anxiously for them to either call us or return. Finally, 'The Terrible Tango' tune chimed. I answered. Santana explained what had happened, and I told him we would wait for them by the pool before hanging up.

The expression on my face likely said it all. "Lexi's gone," I announced to the others. "Carlos found the guard hogtied on the floor in the room. Will, you were right. Whoever did it bribed a hotel staff member."

Will practically leapt out of his chair, his hands wringing together like a mortician who had just heard the dam broke. "Leave it to me!" he exclaimed, striding off.

"Where's he going?" Dan asked.

"I'd say to check with the management, find out who sold us out for thirty pieces of silver," I snarled.

Nick cautioned, "Well, if Al Head and his gang didn't know about you and Santana being in town before, they'll certainly know now."

"I wonder who it was," Bella pondered aloud.

Will was the first to return. As he took his seat, a smirk spread across his face. "It took twenty bucks to get the story and a description. It was the bellhop, alright. The guy said he was a cop ... of course. He was around five-nine, receding hairline, Latino look, well-dressed, more like a gangster than a cop, and he had an obvious scar through his left eyebrow."

"Sonny Rivers," I said.

"I know that dirt bag ... one of Head's henchmen," Will grated.

"Head's man in Hollywood until he conveniently skipped town after my friend was murdered," I added savagely.

Just then, Santana and Max arrived and took their seats. I could tell by the expression on Santana's face that he was furious.

"From the description I got from the guard, it was Sonny Rivers," Santana grumbled.

"Yeah, I convinced the bellhop to spill the beans, and we came to the same conclusion," Will confirmed.

"So, Sonny bought off the bellhop," Santana snarled.

"You know this town, Carlos," Max reminded him.

"Yeah, right. Anyhow, a fifty-spot shut the guard up, so no damage was done there ... but now we can be certain that Al Head knows we're coming for him."

That made me ponder what Head would be thinking. Santana's presence and the way we dealt with Lexi would undoubtedly set off alarm bells. He had to be aware that we were planning a raid. The big question would be, when?

"With everything that's happened, we have to proceed as planned," Dan urged. "If we postpone it, it'll only give him more time to prepare."

"You're right, Dan. Let's eat now and then go to the rooms to finalise the plan. If Max can disable the road camera, we should be good to go," I proposed.

Nick raised his glass for a toast and declared, "To success!"

CHAPTER TWENTY-SIX

W ITH THE KNOWLEDGE that Al Head was likely aware of our intentions, we gathered around Max and his laptop on the coffee table in the hotel room to revise the plan. Will positioned himself on the hotel roof, ready to launch the Cyberhawk drone into the Las Vegas evening sky.

"So, can this thing fly to the exact coordinates you input?" Nick inquired.

"Yeah, the UAV has an autopilot for autonomous flight when needed, GPS, a high-quality and infrared camera, eight rotors, a top speed of sixty miles an hour, can fly up to eighteen hundred feet, and has a flight endurance of a hundred and fifty minutes," Max explained. "I sound like a user manual, but that about covers it."

"What's the estimated time of arrival at the target?" Dan asked.

"Fifteen minutes," Max confirmed, wearing a headset to communicate with Will. "Okay, Will," he continued. "Stand back and countdown to launch."

On the laptop display, we could see that Will had positioned the UAV on the rooftop's sidewall, ready for takeoff. Max pressed a couple of keys on his laptop to activate the motors, then initiated the countdown from five. When he reached zero, he hit the spacebar, and the laptop provided us with a bird's-eye view of the takeoff and the stunning nighttime cityscape of Las Vegas. Max inputted further instructions, and the drone banked, heading straight for the target. It was exhilarating, reminiscent of watching a news report on a military operation in a foreign country. Despite its speed of sixty miles per hour, the few cars we spotted on the road below the drone appeared to be speeding by in comparison.

Before long, a look of anticipation crossed Max's face.

"We're closing in on the coordinates. I'll arm it now," he announced.

"What does it carry?" I quietly asked Dan.

Dan whispered back, "Max told me it packs a 9mm Glock set to auto-fire. It has eight rounds to hit the target."

"What about recoil?" I inquired.

"Yeah, I'm curious to see how it handles that," Dan muttered, raising an eyebrow.

"There it is," Max declared, switching the visuals to infrared. "It stands out like a sore thumb!"

We watched intently as the UAV circled the target.

Max pointed at the screen. "See that little hotspot down there? That's the camera."

Using a joystick on the laptop, he guided the UAV down from five hundred feet until it was level with the camera, then had it hover behind the camera where it couldn't be seen.

"Here we go," he said excitedly, then pressed a key.

There was no sound, of course, but we witnessed a puff of smoke from the gun, followed by the recoil.

"Nope, it hit it, but you can tell from the hotspot that the mother is still active. I'll have to take another shot," Max grumbled.

He needed to circle the camera once more to line up for a steady shot.

"Okay, this time," he snarled and pressed the key.

Another puff of smoke erupted, and this time the camera exploded, causing the hotspot to vanish.

"Got it!" Max growled.

Carlos erupted with praise. "Good shooting, partner!"

"Dat was amazing!" Bella cheered.

"Now, I better get the hell out of Dodge before I encounter any resistance. They'll sure a\s hell know their camera is down," Max barked.

I left Max to bring the drone back and went to the adjacent room to call Gary in Australia. It was time to update him. I closed the door behind me for privacy, sat on the bed, and dialled my cellphone. I got his message bank and left a short report. Just as I ended the call, there was a knock at the door. I opened it and found myself staring down the barrel of a gun.

The man behind the gun ordered, "Not a fucking word. Step out of the room." His tone left no room for defiance. There were two of them, both armed. I didn't recognise them, but their body language made it clear they meant business.

"What's this about?" I demanded, trying to speak loudly enough for the others to hear.

"Shut up and do as I say, or you'll end up in the morgue. Put your hands behind you," he snapped.

I complied, and he handcuffed me. From his actions, it was evident that he was a cop, but the other guy certainly wasn't. If there was a contest for looking like a crook, he'd win hands-down.

"Are you cops? If you are, I'm here on police business," I pleaded.

"Do as you're told. Now move!" The cop pushed me along the corridor to the fire escape, while the other guy opened the fire door. They forced me ahead of them down eight flights of stairs to the basement car park. A black SUV was waiting with the engine running and a driver behind the wheel. They pushed me into the back seat, hopped in beside me, and the vehicle sped out of the car park. I mentally checked my belongings: I was still wearing my pistol, and I had my cell phone. The others wouldn't know I had been abducted. It wasn't a good situation, but my best hope was that once they realised I was missing, Santana could track my phone's signal.

I gritted my teeth and asked, "Where are you taking me?"

"You'll find out," the cop answered. He seemed to be the one doing all the talking. It didn't take long for me to figure out that they were taking me to the ranch. The crook in the front seat dialled a number on his phone.

"Yeah, boss, we have him. Yeah, sure, he's in one piece. We're on our way. You want us to stop and check it?" he spoke into the phone. "Okay."

"Let me take a guess," I growled. "The boss is Al Head, and you're on his payroll."

A sharp move from him was the last thing I remembered before everything went black.

~ ~ ~

I came to with a start, sat up, and immediately felt for my gun. It was gone. I wasn't cuffed and was able to feel a lump on the side of my head the size of an egg. My vision cleared, and through the haze, I could see someone sitting opposite me. His lips were moving, but I couldn't hear what he was saying. The tinnitus finally eased, and his voice cut through.

"Hear me, Stone? I've got your gun ... your phone, and you," he said icily.

"If I end up with a brain tumour after that whack, I'll be sending you the medical tab," I snarled cynically.

Al Head was in the chair opposite me, brandishing the look of a Hollywood bandit: a can of beer in one hand and a thin cigarillo burning in the other. His eyes were jet black, a contrast to the white skin of his face ... maybe not so much a jungle cat as a rattlesnake. The air-conditioning hummed softly, and I could feel the patina of sweat turning cold as it dried on my face.

"Why are you and Santana in Vegas?" he demanded.

"Romance, we grew so close back in L.A. we decided to have a dirty weekend before I split for Sydney."

"I had my suspicions about you, Stone."

He crossed his legs and relaxed back in his armchair. I looked around. We were in a large timber-panelled living room with a high ceiling and big exposed redwood beams. Rawhide furniture, a fireplace, and big ceiling-to-floor windows made it high-class cowboy stuff.

A nod from Al brought footsteps behind me on the tiled floor. It would have hurt to screw my neck around and look, so I waited for whoever it was to arrive.

"Well, if it ain't Sonny Rivers, fancy finding a scumbag like you in an upmarket ranch like this," I said facetiously, using my best cowboy accent.

Rivers smacked me hard across the face.

"Not so cheeky now, huh?" Head crowed. "Sonny, he doesn't want to tell me why he's here. What-cha got to loosen his tongue?"

As usual, Sonny was dressed in a grey suit, this time over a black T. He fumbled in his coat pocket, produced a Swiss army knife, and held it up for Al.

"This has lots of choices," he mumbled, sat on the arm of the lounge, and idly swinging his legs like an agitated cat.

"Looks too complicated for your little brain, Sonny," I said, trying to stir him up. "You read the instructions?" I got a result.

Head's look was one of petulant impatience, while Rivers eyed me with a derisive grin curling his lips.

"It is sharp? You know, sharp enough to say cut his balls off?" Al snapped, with a tight-lipped smirk. "Cut him!" he ordered.

It dawned on me; he meant business. "Hey, this is getting out of hand. Don't let him loose with ideas like that; you know he's not the sharpest tool in the shed," I quipped.

Sonny opened the biggest blade the knife had and felt its edge with his thumb. A smug look crossed his face.

Al rolled his cigar between his forefinger and thumb. "I'll ask you one more time, Stone. Why are you and Santana in Vegas?"

"Alright, alright, but first tell him to put that thing away— he might do someone an injury," I proposed nervously. The only option I had was to keep him talking in the hope the cavalry would soon arrive. There was a pregnant pause, beads of sweat were breaking on my forehead. Finally, Al nodded to Sonny, and he slowly closed the penknife, then lowered himself into a chair.

"We're here to arrest you and Rivers for conspiracy to murder," I admitted.

"What are you, a fuckin' comedian? Who am I supposed to have conspired to kill?" Head snarled, acting amused.

"Carson Kincade, Josh Kovacs, and Malika del Mundo," I rasped.

"Why would I kill Kincade? He was my investor ... Malika was a friend, you know that, and I've never heard of no Josh Kovacs. You're barking up the wrong tree, Stone," he growled, drawing on his cigar and then blowing a thin stream of smoke into the air to watch it evanesce.

Sonny added his two cents' worth, "Anyhow Santana's an L.A. cop, way out of his jurisdiction. He can't make no arrest in Nevada ... he knows that."

"You know who Kovacs is, Sonny?... Mr Stein. Anyhow, I'm not hip to your local laws ... I'm from Australia, remember? I leave all the legal stuff to Santana," I lied. "I'm just here to either get the opal back or do a deal. You know I work for the owner, right?"

"I knew you were no film financier, that's for sure ... What makes you think we've got the fuckin' opal?" Head snarled caustically.

"Let's not beat around the bush, Al. You and I both know Volt got it from me at Malika's house."

Head glanced at Sonny, shrugged his shoulders, and then, gesturing with open sanctimonious hands, asked, "Sonny, who's this guy Volt?"

Sonny mirrored him. "Never heard of him, boss."

"Seems you've got amnesia, Sonny," I snapped. "First, you can't remember Kovacs, even though you killed him ... now you can't remember your accomplice? Do you remember Slim Williams, the cop on your payroll? The guy who kidnapped me with Volt ... your paid assassin? That's who fuckin' Volt is."

"You've been watching too many Tarantino flicks, Stone. You come over here from your little country somewhere in the Pacific, thinking everyone's a freakin' gangster," he barked. "I'm a legitimate businessman." He jumped up out of his chair and began gesturing like he was an emperor showing off his palace. "Take a good look around, Stone ... I started with fuckin' nothing, nothing ... and built all of this from hard work. Now, why would I risk it all by killing those people, huh? Fuckin' ridiculous—what, over some goddamn opal that isn't even worth the asking price? No, no, Stone, you've got the bull by the ass."

"The correct expression is 'the bull by the tail,' Al," I corrected him, trying to regain some control of the situation. "And your sermon of self-importance was exactly what I'd expect from a narcissist—"

"Shut up, Stone! You and your big words... you're nothing but a mouth on a stick," Sonny growled angrily.

I got the impression that the bookends were getting all wound up and were likely to start taking it out on me. But I desperately needed to buy more time ... I needed to needle them some more.

Head slipped behind me ... I heard a rustle, and a belt looped around my throat. I grabbed at it, struggling to get my fingers underneath, but he pulled it so tight it was choking me. No matter how hard I battled, I was tethered. Just when I thought I was about to pass out, he eased off the tension. I gasped for air.

Through gritted teeth, he snarled, "Not so fuckin' smart now, are you, Stone? So, what am I gonna do with you? You gave my opal to some bum, you screwed my girl, you're blaming me for three murders," he grated.

I needed to think of something quick; it was getting ugly. My mind was racing, and I figured the others would know by now that I'd been hijacked and would be on the way. The chopper would arrive soon, provided everything was still going to plan.

"How about we do a deal for the opal?" I rasped.

He slipped the belt from around my throat.

"Are you hard of hearing, smartass?" he eyeballed me and shouted, "I don't have no fuckin' opal!"

It was time to take a risk and use attack as defence or get whacked.

"Let's cut to the chase and dispense with the bullshit, Head. Just before I shot Williams, he blew the whistle on you. He thought it was all over for me, so he couldn't resist blowing his bags. I got the lot. That's what convinced Santana to step out of his territory to arrest you ... now do you get it?"

"You think you're so fuckin' smart, don't you, Stone?" he growled angrily. He was losing his rag again ... he didn't like being pushed into a corner.

I pressed him harder, "Yeah, I'm smart, and I think you, Sonny, and Volt are a bunch of fuckin' clowns, raising money for a movie that you'll never make, nothing more than a cheap scam. Real players like Gerry Mansfield know your number. That's why Malika didn't want to know about your bullshit movie. You're probably doing it all just to keep Lexi ... and why not, I say? Everybody else has her one way or the other. I certainly enjoyed her, and I reckon she loved it..."

That got him. His face flushed red as a beetroot, and he angrily threw his cigar into the fireplace. He picked up the fire poker leaning against the wall and rushed me with it. I grabbed a cushion from the lounge chair and raised it to take the blow. But it never came ... he stopped just short of me with the metal rod raised in the air.

"Sonny!" he growled madly. "Take this bum downstairs and kill him, slowly. Do it now before I beat him to death with this. Get him out of my fuckin' face!" he roared.

Sonny pulled a gun. "Get up, Stone. I'm gonna enjoy this."

CHAPTER TWENTY-SEVEN

I HAD BRAIN-FOG from being half choked to death. Maybe I'd pushed Head a little too far. Rivers poked his gun into my ribs, and that got me out of the armchair quick smart.

"Don't even think about making a run for it, Stone. I'm a damn good shot."

"Yeah, I've seen evidence of that," I snarled.

He shoved me in the back and almost pushed me over. We left Head leaning with both his hands against the mantle of the big fireplace, brooding. Sonny prodded me along a dark corridor with a parquet floor and timber-paneled walls.

"Take the stairs on your left," he barked.

"Where are we going?"

"Shut up," he snapped and shoved me in the back. It was becoming a habit with him, and I was longing for the opportunity to smack him in the mouth. I turned into a staircase that led down into darkness and stopped. He hit a switch beside the doorway, and a light illuminated a dozen steps down to the basement. Another stab in the ribs with the gun forced me down them. He stopped me at the base in front of a big bolted stainless-steel door. With the gun trained on me, he slid open the heavy bolt and then pressed the light switch on the wall before swinging the heavy door open.

"Inside!" he snarled.

It was a cold room, and it lived up to its name—it was freezing. The shelves were laden with frozen pre-packed food, and two pig carcasses were suspended on meat hooks from a ceiling rail. A dozen large sacks of what looked like potatoes were stacked in the corner at the far end of the twenty-by-ten-feet room.

"Looks like Al shops in bulk," I joked, my breath vaporising in the cold.

"Very funny, but the last laugh's on you, pal, 'coz you're looking at your morgue."

Keeping his gun on me, he bent down and untied a string around one end of a sack of potatoes and then jerked it open.

"See what I mean?" he pointed at the contents. I looked inside into the lifeless eyes of Lexi Diamond, staring up at me with frozen white eyes, in silent terror. Her mouth was agape in a rictus of agony with a coating of frost on her tongue and eyebrows.

"The boss don't like being cheated on," he sniggered.

It was now or never because Sonny was going to put a bullet in me any second. In a flash, I grabbed a pig carcass and swung it at him with all my might. The sound of the gun firing in the close confines of the room was deafening. Rivers couldn't withstand the momentum of the swinging pig cannoning into him. He grunted painfully as he cartwheeled backward and landed hard on the sacks of potatoes and Lexi. The impact jolted the gun out of his hand, and it slid across the wet floor. I dived for it, scooped it up, got to my feet, dashed for the freezer door, got out, slammed it shut, and rammed home the bolt. Puffing, I leaned against the door. It had been way too close for comfort. As a last touch, I switched off the light inside so that Sonny would have to deal with the dark as well as the freezing cold ... I could hear his muffled screams of terror from inside the freezer.

"Just chill with Lexi, Sonny boy," I growled loud enough for him to hear, and then headed up the staircase.

Caution was required. I wasn't familiar with the layout of the house, even though Dan had walked us through the floor plan. It's a lot different when you're in it and armed, not knowing whether or not your adversary is around the next corner, brandishing a shotgun. I planned to head back to the living room, hoping Head would still be there waiting for Sonny. Then I heard a familiar beating sound—the chopper—the troops had arrived. As I skirted the corridor with the gun up and ready, I expected at any moment to hear the vehicles crash through the front gates as planned, but heard nothing. Then, all hell broke loose ... it was as though World War III had erupted outside. Pressed hard against the corridor wall, I peeped around the corner into the living room, looking for Al, but he wasn't there. Through the big windows, I could vaguely make out the outline of a white chopper with muzzle flashes coming from it. Lots of gunshots. I wasn't sure which were friendly or foe, but whatever—it was intense. Out of the corner of my eye, I caught sight of movement. Someone was scurrying up the staircase to the second floor. It must be Head. From up there, he could easily pick off my guys in the courtyard. I needed to go after him.

I raced over to the staircase, ran up, and onto the landing at the top, then stopped to listen for footsteps. But the carpeted floor meant there were none to hear. The lights were out, it was dim—rooms on either side of the long hallway—it would be potluck figuring out which one Head had entered. The most logical room would be facing the courtyard. I needed to move fast. Even if he got off one shot, it might well be fatal for one of my buddies.

Nervously, I reached for the door handle to the first of three doors, gave it a gentle turn, and it opened. I waited, and then took a quick peek inside. It was a bedroom. No-one there. I raced to the next door and repeated the action. It was another vacated bedroom. The last room at the end of the hallway had to be the master bedroom, and my money was on finding him there. The gunfight was continuing outside with fewer shots than before ... I hoped that was because we were winning. I leaned up against the door and gently turned the handle. It clicked—locked. No going back now. I stood back and kicked it, once—twice—the third kick punched it open. I was expecting gunfire from within, but when nothing came, gun up, I stormed inside.

It was a big bedroom with a door at the end that I could see a light under. Again, the door was locked. This time, my first kick was strong enough to smash it open. No sooner had it opened than I realised three more doorways were on the other side. I didn't muck around and kicked the first one open, whether it was locked or not. A Jacuzzi was on the other side. I bypassed the next door because I could see light under the one after that and gave it a massive kick. It flew open. On the other side was the open heavy door to a walk-in safe, and a staircase leading down to what I guessed to be the garage. The floor of the safe was littered with documents. It was obvious Head had been in a big hurry to clean it out and bail. I heard a car start up in the garage below.

He was going to make a run for it! Without any thought of self-preservation, I raced down the stairs just in time to see a grey Cadillac CTS-V backing out of the double garage. I leaned up against the Pajero in the other car space, took aim, fired, and took out the two front tyres. The Caddy stopped in a big hurry, and a cloud of dust swamped the headlights, obscuring the vehicle. It was difficult to make out whether Head had gotten out or not, but when he opened fire, it was obvious he'd taken cover behind the crippled Caddy.

"Come out with your hands up, Al. This doesn't have to end ugly!" I yelled, hoping he'd surrender.

"Come get me, Stone!" he bellowed.

The gunfire in the courtyard ceased; someone had won the battle. I hoped it was my team. A loud shot shook me, and the Caddy exploded in a massive fireball. The percussion pushed me backward, and I felt the heat on my face. Then, with the arm of his coat ablaze, Head stepped out from behind what was left of the Caddy and walked toward me through the smoke, firing. I stepped out, and like a pair of Western gunslingers from a bygone era, bathed in the flickering amber glow of the flaming vehicle, we squared off sixty feet apart, turned side-on, and fired. Bullets whizzed past my ears and struck the garage door at my back, letting out a loud, chilling, metallic wallop. I kept firing. I hit him, and he dropped to one knee. As I walked toward him, he raised his gun to fire, so I let him have it again, this time in the face. He collapsed, a pile of trembling flesh. Standing over his quivering body, looking down at the wretched man ... the flinching suddenly ceased. His black hair was plastered to his scalp with blood. His lips were drawn back over his white teeth, set in a silent snarl. The first hit had made a gory mess of his clothes. His face was unrecognisable: the last shot had taken out his right eye and half the cheekbone. The remaining smoky brown eye stared up at me with glazed hatred.

It was over ... I heard footsteps behind, turned sharply, and found Nick.

"Axis! You alright?" he yelled, puffing out of breath. He stopped beside me and looked down at the body. "Is that who I think it is?"

"There lies a murderer steeped in the colour of his trade," I growled.

"Ah, Al Head, no doubt ... and this?" Nick said as he bent down and picked up an old-fashioned carpetbag that lay beside Head's body. He unclipped it and peered inside. "It's full of money."

"Hand it over for a sec," I said quickly.

I checked. There must have been a couple of mil in stacks of hundred-dollar bills. I helped myself to twenty-five bundles, shoved them into my pockets, and then clipped the bag shut. "For what Gary is owed for the opal," I growled.

Nick grinned at me agreeably.

Dan ambled up with an M16 slung over his shoulder.

"Great shot, Dan. Sure made a bloody mess of the Caddy. What was it?" I asked.

"A grenade," he said, with a proud smirk.

"Where are the rest of the guys?" I asked.

Dan looked down at the bloody mess at our feet and said, "Bella and Santana are guarding four prisoners. Max and Will never made it."

"What!" I exclaimed, thinking them dead.

"Santana said as they approached the ranch, he saw their car roll over. He couldn't stop to help. We just hope they're okay," Nick said.

I collected the bag, and then Dan led us around to the rear of the ranch house where he expected to find Bella and Santana.

"How many casualties, Nick?" I asked along the way.

"Provided Will and Max are okay, none on our side, but they lost one and another is wounded."

"And Head, so that's two dead," I said.

"And there's another one holed up in the barn. We still need to be careful," Dan warned.

We rounded the side of the house, and Dan quickly led us inside through the rear door. Santana and Bella were in the living room with the prisoners.

"Axis, you're alive. Good thing we decided to hit the place early," Santana said.

"I'm happier about that than you. It was looking pretty grim for a while," I admitted.

"God, we were so worried about you, darling," Bella told me, keeping her gun trained on the two handcuffed prisoners sitting cross-legged on the floor.

"Where's Head?" Santana asked.

"Bought the farm," I said whimsically.

He added, "And Rivers?"

"Oh, forgot about him. He's downstairs in the freezer room with Lexi," I reported.

"Dead or alive?" Santana asked.

"Lexi's dead. Head killed her, and Sonny would be near to meeting his maker, but I'm in no real hurry to save the bastard."

"We'll need someone to blow the whistle on Head's operation, so Dan, take over here while I go get Rivers," Santana said.

"What about the guy in the barn?" Dan asked.

"He's for the meat wagon," Santana grinned. "Bella got him with a clean hit. Good shot, ain't you, girl?"

She smiled back at him coyly.

"I'll show you the way," I said and led Carlos into the hallway. "Any word on Max and Will?" I asked along the way.

"Yeah, spoke to them on the phone. They're okay but real pissed for missing the big show."

"No injuries?"

"Battered and bruised."

"What happened?"

"They were following me when a car came out of nowhere and t-boned them. They rolled over. There was a gunfight, but our boys got it done."

We reached the staircase to the cellar and the freezer room. I found the light switch, and we went down.

"Is he armed?" Santana asked.

I held up the 9 mm. "No, I borrowed it. Cover me while I open up." I gripped the bolt, slid it open, and flicked on the interior light.

Rivers was curled up on the floor just inside the door in a foetal position, frosted and out cold. I felt his neck for a pulse.

"Is he alive?" Santana queried.

"Yep. Just. Lexi's in a sack amongst the potatoes."

We dragged Rivers out of the freezer, left him on the floor, and then locked the cellar door from the top of the stairs.

"He'll thaw out soon enough, then we'll pick him up. Right now, I need to go get Max and Will so we can clean up the mess," Santana grated.

CHAPTER TWENTY-EIGHT

S ANTANA HAD FETCHED Will and Max back with us in the Ranch living room.

"I'll make coffee," Bella offered.

"I'll give you a hand," Nick said, and followed her in search of the kitchen.

I handed Santana the carpetbag. "Here, this is what Head was bailing out with ... there's some missing to cover the opal."

"I didn't hear that," Santana said, with a wry smile taking the bag.

We slumped into a couple of black and white cowhide armchairs feeling weary but urgently in need of devising a new exit strategy.

"With Max's car wrecked we'll be needing another vehicle to ferry these bums to jail in Baker," Santana said.

"The Pajero in the garage should do the trick," I figured.

Out of the corner of my eye I saw a flash of white. I jumped up, pulled my gun and took off into the hallway after it. Nick heard me running, popped out of the kitchen and followed. I stopped at a door that was just closing. With my gun held ready, I gently pushed it open and then tentatively stepped inside. It was a small room: a kid's bedroom. After a few seconds I got the uneasy feeling someone was there. When I turned my head, I saw a solemn face peeking at me from behind the door with big grey eyes. She edged towards me clutching a Teddy bear tightly to her chest. Her ankle-length white cotton nightgown was overprinted with little red love hearts. Her cute face was framed with a beautiful shock of long black hair. I guessed she was all of five or six years old.

"Hey there..." I gave her a smile while slyly holstering my gun.

"I'm Samantha," she announced coyly. "Where's my Daddy?"

"What's your Daddy's name darling?"

"This is my Daddy's house, who are you? All the noise was scary."

The notion that Al Head had a daughter nearly floored me — he didn't seem the type.

"Where is your mommy, Samantha?" Nick asked gently from behind me.

"I don't have a mommy, only a daddy ... but I do have Snowy," she said holding out the Teddy Bear for us to see.

Luckily Bella pushed past me, went to Samantha and rescued me from an awkward situation. I'm not great with little ones.

Crouching to get level with the little girl Bella said warmly, "Hello, I heard you say your name is Samantha, zat's a pretty name. My name is Bella and dese are my friends."

"Thank you, Bella," I whispered softly.

"Leave her with me guys, ze coffee is in ze living room."

"You talk funny Bella, but I like it. Wanna see my room?" Samantha said cutely.

We left knowing it was better to leave her with the kid besides, I was overcome with guilt after having blown her father to kingdom come.

When Nick and I got back to the living room Max told me Santana and Will had gone to get Rivers. We sat down for a coffee. It was getting late and we needed the caffeine hit to keep us going. My head felt like it was full of cotton wool after everything that had happened.

A few minutes later Santana and Will arrived with Rivers, handcuffed and looking a worse for wear from his ordeal.

"Hey Sonny boy, off the ice now? You look chilled," I quipped facetiously.

He snarled at me. Will took him over to the other prisoners seated on the floor.

Santana handed me a cellphone. "It's Sonny's, he's been making calls while he was thawing out in the basement but he won't say to who ... my guess is the cavalry ... we should've frisked him."

"Are you expecting an attack?" I asked.

"Not now, I gave him his phone back and told him to call whoever he'd phoned, tell them everything's fine, otherwise if someone arrives I'd put the first slug in him."

"Did he oblige?"

"Yep, but I still don't trust the bastard," he growled, and then gave Rivers a stink-eye.

I filled Carlos in on Samantha. Her arrival had added to his dilemma, with a minor involved he had no choice but to call it in to the Nevada police. Max and Will agreed.

"Forget the plan," Santana said solemnly. "We need to rethink the whole deal. First of all, the contents of the bag will be the child's inheritance if there's nothing else. Next, we need to work out how to get out of this without ending up in the shit."

"I've got an idea," Will said, confidently.

I left Will, Max and Santana to sort it, there wasn't much I could add: local law enforcement was well out of my league. I went with Dan and Nick to check on the chopper. Dan was concerned it might have taken a bullet or two from the gunfight.

We gave it a good going over and found nothing. Just as we finished, Santana joined us.

"The bird okay?" he rasped.

"Seems so," I said optimistically.

"We've sorted out what we're going to do, it'll take some talking but we don't have much choice. Will and Max have agreed to open dialogue with a couple of their buddies high up in the Vegas force, in the meantime I'll head back to L.A. with Bella, who by the way told me she wants to legally adopt Samantha."

"Whoa! that's one helluver undertaking," I gasped.

"She wants to talk to you. But first I wanted to give you this Nick," he said handing Nick a plastic garbage bag. "There's two hundred large in here to cover the chopper and Dan's costs. I figure Al Head should pick up the tab."

"Thanks Chuck, that'll do nicely," Nick said.

"You better crank that thing up and get the hell outa Dodge," he boomed, and then shook hands with Nick and Dan.

I wandered back inside to say cheerio to Bella. Max and Will met me at the door. We shook hands.

I told them Carlos had my number to give me a call if ever they felt like dropping in to Oz. I went looking for Bella and found her in the kitchen making a cup of hot chocolate for Samantha. It wasn't difficult to recognise they belonged together, Samantha even looked like Bella, same black hair, tanned skin and big eyes.

"Hey ladies, it's time for uncle Axis to fly away."

Bella looked sharply at me like I'd just pinched her wallet. I guess Samantha had been distracting her from reality. With tears welling up in her eyes, she threw her arms around my neck and kissed me passionately.

"Carlos said you're thinking of adopting the little one," I said conspiratorially, so Samantha couldn't hear.

"Yes, do you think it is a good idea?"

"Only you can answer that, love, but looking at the two of you together, absolutely."

She hugged me again.

"Oh Axis, I am really going to miss you."

"And I'll miss you, baby ... but hey, I'll only be a phone call away, and once the dust has settled, I'll come stay a while with you guys, what do you say?"

I glanced at little Samantha hugging Snowy. She ambled over to me and gently caressed my thigh. I bent down and kissed her on the cheek.

"Don't forget uncle Axis, all right?"

"No, I won't, I promise," she purred shyly.

"Wait," I said, pulling out my cellphone. I picked Samantha up, held up my phone, and snapped a selfie of the three of us. "There, that'll give me something to look at whenever I'm lonely."

I felt like I was leaving behind the girl I loved when I walked out of that kitchen. All the way back outside, I spent convincing myself that it wasn't so, even though I knew otherwise. It was the first time I'd fallen totally in love.

When I reached the chopper, Nick looked me in the eye and said with uncanny perception, "Hmm, if I didn't know any better, I'd say Mr Stone is suffering from rubber glove."

"You're absolutely right, my friend. You don't know any better," I turned to Santana. "Well, Carlos, I feel like I'm leaving you with a pile of shit to clean up, but hey, we got the job done, didn't we?"

He pulled me into a big Latino bear hug and affectionately slapped me on the back. "It's been real nice working with you, Axis."

"Are you sure you're going to be all right? I don't like leaving unfinished business."

"We'll be just fine. I'll get on the road with Bella pretty well as soon as you take off ... call me when you get to Frisco. You hear me?"

~ ~ ~

Two hours later, we were at San Francisco International Airport. It was just after 6 a.m., we had time to kill ... the flight to Sydney wasn't leaving until 2 p.m.

'The Terrible Tango' sounded. It was Santana. I put him on speaker for Nick and Dan to hear.

"Carlos, how goes it? Tell me you're safely on the road to L.A."

"Yeah, it was a little difficult for Samantha to let go of Bella, but Will is looking after her. Look, I think there might be a complication."

"Yeah, how is that?"

"I found your number in Rivers' phone book. Remember I said the Stingray picked up Lexi making a call just after you met her?"

"Yup."

"We know she called Rivers to meet her, but she also gave him your number."

"How did she get that?"

"I don't know, but it's in his phone."

"Why is that a problem?" I queried.

"I can see from his call log he phoned Volt, and I reckon it was to give him your number. I'd put my house on him tracking you."

"Sounds a bit sophisticated for a hitman."

"Tracking software is freely available, I reckon he's hip to high tech gadgetry. So, you better trash that phone of yours, then watch your ass. He'll be hunting you for sure, especially when he probably knows you took out Head."

"I hear you ... put me onto Bella, will you, mate?"

"Hello Axis, I am so missing you," she purred.

"Hi baby, yeah, me too ... so it was tough letting go of the little one, huh?"

"Yes, but I promised to see her in a couple of days. I will move heaven and Earth for her, Axis. Rivers told me Lexi was her mother and zat she had been kept a secret for obvious reasons."

"So, her relationship had been going for at least six years with Head. Makes him look even more like a maniac for killing his daughter's mother."

"Dat is very true," her voice sounded soft and sensual. "Ven will I see you again, darling?"

"I'll do a bit of heaven and Earth moving myself to get back to L.A. Santana will let me know when the coast is clear."

"Okay, my dear ... I love you," she said warmly and then kissed the phone.

"Me too," I muttered, unable to bring myself to repeat those forbidden words, especially in front of Nick—I have, after all, a reputation to protect.

"Axis," Santana said, having taken the phone. "I've got your email ad, and I'll keep you posted on proceedings ... be careful, buddy, I don't like Volt being on the loose, and I can't be of much assistance to you from here."

"No worries, Carlos, I've got my bookends with me ... we'll be just fine. Catch you later, mate."

I turned to Nick. "This bloke Anderson Volt is one serious piece of work."

"A pro?"

"Yes, he's the one who mutilated Malika's body, killed Kovacs, and we suspect did Kincade. I guess he figures he's got unfinished business with me."

"Well then, we'll just have to keep you safe for the next eight hours before we board that flight," Dan said with conviction.

I admitted, "I feel vulnerable without a piece. Santana made me surrender it."

"What is this Anderson Volt's MO?" Dan queried.

"As far as I know, a bullet in the back of the head. He's a hitman."

"Execution style," Nick observed.

"Why are you asking, Dan?"

"Trying to think of the safest place to be ... a place where he won't be able to put a bullet in your head," Dan grumbled.

"We can go to the airport business class lounge at 11 a.m. So, all we need to do is find a safe haven until then," Nick proposed.

"And that is not here," Dan said sternly.

The thought of Volt on the prowl made my skin crawl. I hated not being armed.

"Look, if it's an endgame he wants, then that's what he'll bloody-well get," I growled.

CHAPTER TWENTY-NINE

I WASN'T COMPLETELY sure what I meant in my tirade to Nick and Dan, but Nick took it as a stroke of genius.

"Great idea, flush him out, that way we can deal with him. One thing we have in our favour is he doesn't know Dan and I exist," Nick concluded pensively.

"I seriously want to punish this bastard ... You with us, Dan?"

"No need to ask that," he said with a big gold-toothed grin.

"What are your thoughts?" I asked him.

"Somewhere in the city, we split up but follow you to draw him to a tourist location where there will be too many people for him to shoot you. He'll be forced to try and snatch you at gunpoint into a vehicle ... well, that's what I'd do," Dan rasped.

"You're on the money, Dan," I agreed.

Over the next few minutes, we settled on a course of action.

"We'll need to be armed," Nick warned.

"Wait a minute, this dude's a pro—"

Dan cut me off. "And so are we ... So?"

"Okay, I'm just thinking of other options, and there aren't any ... fine, where do we get weapons?"

We stored our bags in an airport locker and then jumped a cab to Union Street in the city. From there, Nick led us into The Collectors Cave, which was just opening its doors for business.

After twenty minutes, we emerged from the shop, each of us packing a replica 9mm Glock.

"Amazing what forty bucks can buy you these days," Nick chuckled, patting the gun concealed inside his jacket pocket.

"How the hell did you know about that place, Nick?" I asked, intrigued.

"I've got a thing about toy stores," he admitted. "I'll tell you about it sometime, but you've got to admit they look the real deal."

Nick wasn't wrong. You could pull one on a cop, and he'd never know the difference. We split up and hopped a cable car to The Point Café at Fisherman's Wharf.

I'd chosen to ignore Santana's advice to ditch my phone. We needed it to lure our catch, and Fisherman's Wharf seemed the perfect location.

I stepped off the cable car and walked along North Point Street to the Point Café. A sunny warm day ... in fact, the San Francisco weather reminded me of Sydney. I sat down in the alfresco section of the café. There were fifteen tables, and being early meant three of them were vacant and far enough apart for us to maintain our anonymity. The view of the waterfront was spectacular, but best of all, it gave us a one hundred and eighty-degree panorama to watch for Volt.

I put my cell phone on the table in front of me like I was baiting a trap and then ordered breakfast. A muffin with egg, bacon, cheese, and avocado, and boy, wasn't it delicious. I topped that off with a Lavender Latte, the house specialty Nick had recommended. I'd not tasted anything quite like it before.

The lack of sleep was beginning to catch up with me, so I ordered a double espresso for a reboot. Then, I sighted Anderson Volt getting out of a sedan parked opposite. I fired a sly signal to Nick two tables away, who immediately copied to Dan seated further from us.

A big man, Volt lumbered up the few stairs to the café, making a beeline for me. He pulled up a chair, sat down opposite, and peered at me over the top of his round sunglasses.

"We meet again, Stone," he growled expressionlessly.

"I don't recall inviting you to sit at my table, Volt," I returned serve with interest.

I heard a click under the table.

"That was me cocking my pistol ... it is aimed at your balls. If you want to keep them, then you'll leave payment for your food on the table, stand slowly, and accompany me to my car."

"And why would I want to do that? I don't think you're going to shoot me in full view of the patrons," I tested.

"If you're willing to take the risk, then so am I," he said smoothly. "You see, unlike you, I'm experienced at doing this kind of crap."

"I don't doubt it, but before we go, how about a little chat. Why do you want to kill me?"

"Who said anything about killing you?"

"Surely you didn't go to all this trouble to track me down just to hold hands?"

I was buying time for Dan to make his way over to Volt's car and for Nick to pay his bill and get set to follow me. I handed the waitress fifty and told her to keep the change. She gave me a look of doom, obviously not impressed with the five-dollar tip.

"I finish what I start..." Volt said soberly.

I cut him off sharply. "Where's the opal you pinched from me?"

"The one you stole from us? It is back where it belongs."

"If you have the opal, then what's your beef?" I questioned rigidly.

He leaned forward and glared at me over his sunglasses with eyes like a shark. "You killed someone important, and that costs. Now get up, enough talking," he grated.

Remembering I had a toy gun as my only defence, I was overcome with a feeling of insecurity. "Okay, okay, keep your wig on," I countered, bluffing.

It was now or never. I stood up—he copied, and then we made our way towards his car across the street. I could sense Nick wasn't far behind, and I could see Dan loitering near Volt's car. I glanced at Volt ... his right hand was in the side pocket of his black khaki duffle coat, holding the gun on me. I needed to distract him from Dan and Nick.

"You've got a quarter-million-dollar opal, why don't you flog it and go on a holiday? You want another murder on your conscience?" I asserted.

"Don't have no conscience," he snarled.

I should have expected the answer. When we reached the car, he pressed the remote on his key ring, stood beside the front passenger side door, and ordered, "Open it and get in."

I caught the reflection in the car enamel of Dan making his move up behind Volt. I reached for the door handle, pulled the door open, and as I moved, I feigned getting in but instead grabbed Volt's right arm. The timing couldn't have been better.

Dan pressed his toy gun into the middle of Volt's back and snarled, "Hands in the air or you're dead!"

Then another call bellowed from Nick. "I've got you covered, Volt. Do what he says!"

Volt was surrounded. He knew we had him done and slowly raised his hands.

I quickly reached into his pocket, took his gun, and held it on him, glad to have a real one.

Dan patted him down — he was clean.

"Give me the keys!" I commanded.

He handed them over.

"Open the back door!" I growled.

He complied.

I handed the keys to Nick but kept the gun on Volt while he slid into the back seat. I slipped in beside him, keeping the gun pressed hard against his ribs. Dan squeezed in on the other side, so we had him sandwiched between us. Nick climbed in behind the wheel, started the car, and drove off.

We sat in silence for the sixteen miles from Fisherman's Wharf to San Francisco International Airport.

~ ~ ~

Nick turned off the 101 into the airport and found the entrance to the long-term car park on San Bruno Avenue. He took a ticket and then drove us down the spiralling ramp to the bottom floor of the underground facility. He found a park in a dark corner of the gloomy, dimly lit, grey concrete chamber.

After Dan got out, I pushed the gun into Volt's ribs. "Stay there," I growled, and then got out, keeping the gun trained on him. "Okay, out! With your hands up."

I heard Dan open the trunk. It was all going according to plan, but just as Volt was getting out, he let go of an unexpected sharp, solid punch to my gut. I doubled up in pain, sucking in deep breaths, but managed to straighten up quickly. I lifted the gun sharply and belted him under the chin with it as hard as I could. It knocked him backwards and left him holding a bleeding mouth, spitting out blood and broken teeth, but I hadn't knocked him out. He'd never know what hit him next — Dan let fly with a tyre lever he'd taken from the trunk and split Volt's forehead open. His legs crumbled, and he went down like a sack of potatoes. The three of us quickly manhandled him into the trunk.

"Enjoy your stay, Volt," I growled, "the punishment fits the crime."

We threw our toy guns into the trunk with him, and I slammed the hatch shut. I wiped his gun free of prints, went to the passenger seat, and opened the glove compartment. Just as I was about to stash the gun inside, I noticed a familiar piece of rag. I took it out and unfurled it.

"The Pride!" I exclaimed in shock. "Nick, check this out."

He came over, and I placed it in his hand. "The Pride of Queensland, the opal that has caused us so much trouble ... it was in the bloody glove compartment."

Nick stared at it in his hand. It was glowing with radiance even in the dim light.

"Magnificent," he mumbled.

I stashed the gun, closed the glove box, and locked the car but held onto the keys to dispose of later.

"I'll text Santana where to find Volt. A job well done, fellas," I said.

It was only walking distance to International Terminal A. On the way, I thought how lucky I was — we'd gotten the opal back for Gary and Rod, I'd scored a quarter of a million US bucks in cash, plus the bike and an inheritance from Malika. Nick got his expenses covered plus change, Dan got paid, Al got his, Sonny and Volt were to be incarcerated — it was indeed a job well done.

We made for the lockers, redeemed our stuff. I sent Santana the text message, and then I pulled the SIM and ditched it along with Volt's car keys into the nearest trash bin.

"Time to pamper ourselves in the Qantas lounge, guys," Nick said with a tired sigh.

~ ~ ~

As the Dreamliner 787-9 soared out of the clouds into clear blue sky, reclining in a spacious first-class seat, I found myself reminiscing about Kovacs, his infectious laughter, his dry wit, and his captivating Eastern European accent. That led me to reflect on Malika's enchanting accent, her beautiful face and radiant smile imprinted in my memory. I hoped that image would remain with me forever.

Interrupting my thoughts, a flight attendant handed me a glass of JD. I flashed her a charming smile, which earned me a positive response. It also earned me an elbow in the ribs from Nick, seated beside me.

"I thought you were smitten with Bella," he muttered knowingly.

I took a sip of JD and grinned. "I'm always in love, mate."

Nick raised his glass in a toast. "I'll drink to that. By the way, where is the Pride?"

"The smuggler's hole."

Furrowing his eyebrows, Nick asked, "The what?"

I decided to keep it a secret, a special homage to Josh Kovacs. With a wry smile, I replied, "Let's just say it's in a special place. So, mate, another one bites the dust."

Nick nodded in agreement. "Yes indeed, you've chalked up another win for the good guys ... you're certainly in fine form my friend ... So, what's next Kemosabe?"

The End

Don't miss the next thrilling adventure in book four:

CAN OF WORMS

www.ingramcontent.com/pod-product-compliance
Lightning Source LLC
Chambersburg PA
CBHW052017030426

42335CB00026B/3173